ENGLISH CONNECT 365+

ERIC THOMPSON

PARTRIDGE
A Penguin Random House Company

To order additional copies of this book, contact
Toll Free 800 101 2657 (Singapore)
Toll Free 1 800 81 7340 (Malaysia)
orders.singapore@partridgepublishing.com

www.partridgepublishing.com/singapore

1. LAZY

Meaning; Does not like to work hard or does not like to be active.

Examples
1: She won't work, she's too lazy.
2: I've never seen such a lazy person before. He lies in bed all day and does nothing.

Try to find the meaning of this word in a dictionary. Then make your own sentences.

1. _____

_____

2. _____

_____

3. _____

_____

4. _____

_____

5. _____

_____

2. ILL

Meaning: Not well or unhealthy

Examples:
1. I'm not going to work tomorrow. I'm ill and the doctor told me to stay in bed.
2. You're ill several times a year. It's time to go to the doctor.

Try to find other ways of using this word in your dictionary. Then make your own sentences.

1. _____
2. _____
3. _____

3. FEVER

Meanings:
(a) It is a body temperature that is higher than normal
(b) It may also mean a state of excited emotion or activity

Examples:
1. Doctor, I am having a headache, fever and cough. Am I having flu?
2. The whole city seems to be in the football fever of EURO 2012.

Now look it up in a dictionary and make your own sentences.

1. _____
2. _____
3. _____

4. CROSS

Meaning: to go from one side of (something) to the other

Examples
1. He was the first runner to *cross* the finish line.
2. The hunters took 5 days to cross the forest.

Try to look it up for more meanings in your dictionary. Make more sentences.

1. _____
2. _____
3. _____

5. BRIDGE

Meanings;
(a) A structure built over something (such as a river) so that people or vehicles can get across
(b) something that joins or connects different people or things

Examples of potential use:
1. Let's cross the river here. I think it's the only *bridge* in the village.
2. Her work serves as a *bridge* between the past and the present.

Try to look the word up in your dictionary for more meanings and make your own sentences.

1. _____
2. _____
3. _____

6. TO BURN

Meanings; To destroy or damage something by fire or heat

Examples of potential use:
1. The fire started at 6 p.m. and the whole city was burning after only 4 hours.
2. If you play with the matches, you will burn yourself!

Try to look it up in a dictionary and make your own sentences in the spaces below.

1. _____
2. _____
3. _____

7. ECONOMY.

Meaning; The process or system by which goods and services are produced, sold, and bought in a country or region.

Examples of potential use:
1. The government should improve the state of the economy.
2. The high unemployment resulted from the economy crisis of 2008-09.

Look it up in your dictionary for more meanings and examples and make your own sentences in the spaces below.

1. _____
2. _____
3. _____

{Treasure box 1: Make <u>at least</u> one sentence of your own. }

8. TECHNIQUE

Meaning; A way of doing something by using special knowledge or skill.

Examples of potential use:
1. I want to practice some new photographic technique.
2. Psychologists develop new learning techniques.

Now look it up and make our own sentences in the spaces below.

1. _____
2. _____
3. _____

9. COMPLIMENT

Meaning; A remark that says something good about someone or something

Examples of potential use:
1. What a lovely dress! Oh, thanks for the compliment.
2. He couldn't take his eyes off her and was telling her many compliments at the party.

Look it up for more examples and make yours in the spaces below

1. _____
2. _____
3. _____

10. SMOKE

Meaning; the cloud of black, gray, or white gases and dust that is produced by burning something

Examples of potential use:
1. There was a lot of smoke coming from the bonfire made by our neighbors.
2. Do you mind if I smoke here? No, I'd rather you go out, I can't stand the cigarette smoke.

Look up the word in your dictionary and make your own sentences below.

1. _____
2. _____
3. _____

REVIEW: 1

Review with this exercise.

Choose the correct definition for the words below:

1. Fever.
    a. Hostile or unfriendly.
    b. A rise in the temperature of the body; frequently a symptom of infection.
    c. Something that reflects in an unfavorable way on one.

2. Economy.
    a. Intense nervous anticipation; "in a fever of resentment.
    b. The system of production and distribution and consumption
    c. Something that reflects in an unfavorable way on one.

3. Smoke.
    a. Something that causes suffering.
    b. Something that reflects in an unfavorable way on one.
    c. A cloud of fine particles suspended in a gas.

4. To survive.
    a. Continue to live through hardship or adversity.
    b. Resulting in suffering.
    c. To separate into components or parts.

5. Ill
    a. To exist or support oneself.
    b. To cause to separate into pieces suddenly or violently.
    c. Not healthy or sick.

6. To burn.
   a. To undergo rapid combustion or consume fuel in such a way as to give off heat.
   b. Continue to live through hardship or adversity.
   c. To cause to separate into pieces suddenly or violently.

7. Technique.
   a. To live past a life-threatening event.
   b. To feel strong emotion or passion.
   c. A practical method or art applied to some particular task.

8. Bridge.
   a. A specific method of production.
   b. A structure that allows people or vehicles to cross an obstacle such as a river or canal or railway etc.
   c. To force or make a way through, puncture or penetrate.

9. To cross.
   a. To connect or reduce the distance between objects.
   b. To intersect or meet at a point.
   c. To force or make a way through , puncture or penetrate.

10. Sudden.
    a. To feel extreme anger.
    b. To become separated into pieces or fragments.
    c. Happening without warning or in a short space of time.

11. TO NOTICE

Examples of potential use:
1. She had a new blouse, but her husband didn't even notice it.
2. I noticed that they were looking rather nervous and asked them what had happened.

Try to find what the meaning of this word is using these examples and a good dictionary and make your own sentences below.

1. _____
2. _____
3. _____

12. STRANGER

MEANING
One who is neither a friend nor an acquaintance.

Examples of potential use:
1. A tall, dark-skinned stranger waved to me in front of the shop. Do you know him?
2. The quietness of the village was disturbed by the arrival of the stranger from an unknown land.

Try to find the meaning of this word using these examples and a good dictionary and make your own sentences below.

1. _____
2. _____
3. _____

13. BREAK

MEANING
To cause separation into pieces suddenly or violently.

Examples of potential use:
1. I dropped the glasses and they all broke, making a lot of noise and mess.
2. They died in the mountains when their rope suddenly broke.

Try to find the meaning of this word using these examples and a good dictionary. Now make your own sentences below.

1. _____

2. _____

3. _____

14. SPEAK UP

MEANINGS
1. **To speak loud enough to be audible.**
2. **To speak without fear or hesitation.**

Examples of potential use.
1. Speak up please, because people at the back don't hear you.
2. If you disagree with the others, you should speak up now.

Try to find the meaning of this word using these examples and a good dictionary.

Now make your own sentences below.

1. _____

2. _____

3. _____

- {Treasure box 2; *I strongly recommend using a paper English-English dictionary* when you study on your own. Many teachers have noticed that their students remember words much longer when they search for them in the paper dictionary. Also, dictionaries in book form generally give more detail examples than electronic dictionaries.}

15. SUDDEN

Meaning; something is sudden when it is happening, coming, or done very quickly in a way that is usually not expected.

Examples of potential use:
1. His sudden illness made us cancel our trip to Paris.
2. There was a sudden increase in the price of oil.

Try to look it up in the dictionary for more examples and make your own sentences below.

1. _____
2. _____
3. _____

16. TO RECOMMEND

Meanings; When you recommend something or someone you say that someone or something is good and deserves to be chosen.

Examples of potential use:
1. Can you recommend me a good place to go on holidays?
2. I recommend that you read this book if you want to pass the exam. You'll find the most important facts there.

Look the meaning up in a dictionary for more understanding and make your own sentences below.

1. _____
2. _____
3. _____

17. SURVIVE

MEANING:
To remain alive or in existence.

Examples of potential use:
1. Four people were killed in the accident; she was the only one to survive.
2. They somehow managed to survive the difficult time of the war.

Try to find the meaning of this word using these examples and a good dictionary.

Now make your own sentences below.
1. _____
2. _____
3. _____

18. DECLARE

Meaning:
To make something known formally or officially or to say something in a strong and confident way.

Examples of potential use:
1. Do you have anything to *declare*?
2. She was declared the winner of the first prize.

Try to find the meaning of this word using these examples and a dictionary.

Now make your own sentences below.
1. _____
2. _____
3. _____

19. RICH

Meaning:

To have great abundant supply of something or to possess great material wealth.

Examples of potential use:
1. She married him, because he's rich and able to give her everything she'd always dreamt about.
2. Fruits are rich in vitamins.

Try to find the meaning of this word using these examples and a good dictionary.

Now make your own sentences below.
1. _____
2. _____
3. _____

20. INSERT

Meaning:

To put something in something.

Examples of potential use:
1. The light went out and I had difficulties to insert the key in the lock.
2. She inserted the letter between the books hoping that her husband won't find it.

Try to find the meaning of this word by using these examples and a good dictionary.

Now make your own sentences below.

1. _____

2. _____

3. _____

REVIEW: 2

Choose the best words for the following definitions:

1. A movement from one place to another.
   a. Fever
   b. To notice
   c. Cross
   d. Ill

2. A warning or intimation of something.
   a. Technique
   b. Smoke
   c To notice
   d. Sudden

3. An expression of esteem, respect, affection, or admiration.
   a. Compliment
   b. Stranger
   c. To recommend
   d. To survive.

4. A person or thing that is unknown or with whom one is unacquainted.
   a. Compliment.
   b. Stranger
   c. Economy
   d. Rich

5. To present as worthy of acceptance or trial.
   a. Rich
   b. Recommend
   c. To survive
   d. To assist.

6. To convey thoughts, opinions, or emotions orally.
   a. To insert
   b. To speak up
   c. To notice
   d. To break

7. To make known formally or officially.
   a. To assist
   b. To insert
   c. To declare
   d. To compliment

8. To give aid or support.
   a. To cross
   b. To burn
   c. To hire
   d. To speak up.

9. Possessing great material wealth.
   a. Hire
   b. Assist
   c. Rich
   d. Brand

10. Payment for labor or services to a worker, especially remuneration on an hourly daily or weekly basis or by the piece.
    a. Hire
    b. Wage
    c. Quality
    d. Consult

21. QUALITY

Meaning:
How good or bad something is.

Examples of potential use:
1. I won't visit this restaurant again. The food is of such a poor quality.
2. If you buy top quality products with a lifelong guarantee, you have to pay more.

Try to find the meaning of this word using these examples and a good dictionary.

Treasure box 3:
{When you discuss in English, you need to imagine a lot and avoid translating into your native language in your head to be able to keep up with your discussion.}

22. ASSIST

Meaning:
To give support or help

Examples of potential use:
1. We are expected to assist the guests with interpreting during the conference and their free time.
2. Foreign armies arrived to assist in restoring peace.

Try to find the meaning of this word using these examples and a good dictionary.

Now make your own sentences below.
1. _____
2. _____
3. _____

23. HIRE

<u>Meaning:</u>
To give work or a job to (someone) in exchange for wages or a salary

<u>Examples</u> of potential use:
1. How much does it cost to hire a car for 2 days?
2. He was hired for a short period of time to help with the new project.

Try to find the meaning of this word using these examples and a dictionary.

Now make your own sentences below.
1. _____
2. _____
3. _____

24. WAGES

Here are two examples of potential use:
Ex 1.: Graduating from university cannot guarantee high wages nowadays.
Ex 2.: She's too proud to work for low wages.

Try to find the meaning of this word using these examples and a dictionary.

Now make your own sentences below.
1. _____
2. _____
3. _____

25. MULTINATIONAL COMPANIES

Here are two examples of potential use:
1. Many multinational companies set up their subsidiaries in Asia to benefit from its cheap labor force.
2. Multinational companies contribute essentially to globalization.

Try to find the meaning of this word using these examples and a dictionary.

26. COMPETITIVE

Here are two examples of potential use:
1. Football/Soccer is one of the most competitive sports in the world.
2. The market of electronic devices is very competitive because of high innovation.

Try to find the meaning of this word by using these examples and a dictionary.

27. BRAND AWARENESS

Here are two examples of potential use:
1. The key to success is to build brand awareness among customers.
2. People easily associate Nokia with mobile phones and Levis with jeans due to the high brand awareness.

Try to find the meaning of this word by using these examples and a dictionary.

28. CLASSIC BRAND

Here are two examples of potential use:
1. Levis is perceived as a classic brand in the clothing market.
2. People often choose classic brands that they've known for ages, because they seem reliable for them.

Try to find what the meaning of this word is using these examples and a dictionary.

Now make your own sentences below.
1. _____
2. _____
3. _____

Treasure box: 4 {Practice makes perfection; you have to practice as much as you can if you really want to be fluent.}

29. ZEBRA CROSSING

Here are two examples of potential use:
1. Many people die each day, because they don't cross roads on zebra crossing.
2. I failed my driving test, because I forgot to slow down before zebra crossing.

Try to find the meaning of this word using these examples and a dictionary.

30. TO REDUCE

Here are two examples of potential use:
1. Our company really needs to reduce expenses at this difficult time.

2. Many shops reduce their prices before Christmas to attract customers.

Try to find the meaning of this word using these examples and a good dictionary.

{Congratulations, you're on your way to fluency. Now review with this exercise: }

REVIEW: 3

Choose the best word for the following definitions:

1. **H**aving a happy feeling; in good spirits.
   a. Wages
   b. Commercial
   c. Consult
   d. Cheerful

2. To seek advice or information.
   a. To reduce
   b. To consult
   c. To notice
   d. To hire

3. To manufacture or create economic goods and services.
   a. To produce
   b. To reduce
   c. To recommend
   d. To survive

4. Not hypocritical or deceitful; open; genuine.
   a. Competitive
   b. Quality
   c. Sincere
   d. Cruel

5. Free from showiness or ostentation; unpretentious
   a. Assist
   b. Recommend
   c. Modest
   d. Rich.

6. Something useful that can be turned to commercial or other advantage
   a. Commodity.
   b. Commercial
   c. Competitive
   d. Economy

7. To engage the services of (a person) for a fee.
   a. To hire
   b. To assist
   c. To insert
   d. To compliment

8. To put or set into, between, or among.
   a. To hire
   b. To assist
   c. To inset
   d. To speak up

9. Degree or grade of excellence.
   a. Commercial
   b. Quality
   c. Rich
   d. Commodity

10. To bring down amount, or degree; diminish.
    a. To declare
    b. To hug
    c. To produce
    d. To reduce

31. COMMERCIAL

Examples of potential use:
1. What drives me mad while watching films is a commercial break every 20 minutes.
2. Commercials are the main source of media income.

Try to find the meaning of this word using these examples and a dictionary.

Now make your own sentences below.
1. _____
2. _____
3. _____

32. TO CONSULT

Here are two examples of potential use:
1. If you have any problem with the project, please consult our experts.
2. I have no idea of how to get there. I'll consult the map.

33. CHEERFUL

Here are two examples of potential use:
1. In spite of his numerous problems he's always cheerful.
2. After having a bad day I like listening to some cheerful music.

Try to find the meaning of this word using these examples and a dictionary.

34. COMMODITY

Here are two examples of potential use:
1. People are afraid that commodity prices will rise if we enter the Euro zone.
2. Farmers are happy, because the demand for agricultural commodities has risen recently.

Try to find the meaning of this word using these examples and a dictionary.

35. TO PRODUCE

Here are two examples of potential use:
1. His company produces mobile phones.
2. There's a slump in producing luxury goods, because people don't buy as many of them as in the past.

Try to find the meaning of this word using these examples and a dictionary.

TREASURE BOX: Keep it simple and short.

This means that you should not try to explain in long sentences all the time. When you keep it simple and short,

a. You go straight to the point.
b. You will save yourself the headache of explaining.
c. You will not confuse yourself and your listener.
d. You will save your time and your listener's.

36. MODEST

Here are two examples of potential use:
1. She was so modest about her success. She said that it was nothing extraordinary.
2. He's rich but modest. He never makes the other feel worse.

Try to find the meaning of this word using these examples and a dictionary.

37. CRUEL

Here are two examples of potential use:
1. The guards were very cruel to the prisoners.
2. Vegetarians claim that eating animals is cruel.

Try to find the meaning of this word using these examples and a dictionary

38. SINCERE

Here are two examples of potential use:
1. I'm sure he was not sincere in what he said to me last night. He often tells lies.
2. He's a great actor. He's so sincere in what he does!

Try to find the meaning of this word using these examples and a dictionary.

39. QUARREL

Here are two examples of potential use:
1. After a quarrel they decided to split up.

2. Our neighbors quarrel all the time, preventing me from falling asleep.

Try to find the meaning of this word using these examples and a dictionary.

40. ORDINARY

Here are two examples of potential use:
1. They've got an ordinary sort of house, it's really nothing special.
2. People wake up every morning to start another ordinary day.

Try to find what the meaning of this word is using these examples and a dictionary.

REVIEW: 4

Here is the review for some of the words that we have learned

Choose the best word for the following definitions:

1. An angry dispute; a disagreement marked by a temporary or permanent break in friendly relationship.
   a. Cruel
   b. Modest.
   c. Quarrel

2. To deduct a certain amount from a bill, charge, etc.
   a. To reduce
   b. To consult
   c To discount

3. To breathe during sleep with hoarse or harsh sounds.
   a. To survive
   b. To snore
   c. To sneeze

4. To look with winking or half-shut eyes.
   a. Dive
   b. Blink
   c. Examine

5. To actively and attentively engaged in work or a pastime.
   a. Busy
   b. Consult
   c. Assist

6. Something offensive or annoying to individuals or to the community.
   a. Rotten
   b. Quarrel
   c. Nuisance

7. **P**lain or undistinguished.
   a. Assist
   b. Spot
   c. Ordinary

8. A complete in natural growth or development, as plant and animal forms.
   a. Sincere
   b. Mature
   c. Superior

9. **A**n approximate judgment or calculation, as of the value, amount, time, size, or weight of something
   a. Quality
   b. Brand
   c. Estimate

10. To give back or restore, especially money.
    a. Refund
    b. Review
    c. Repeat

41. TO HUG

Here are two examples of potential use:
1. She hugged him tightly, because she really missed him.
2. The mother hugged the child after he apologized to her for his bad behavior.

Try to find what the meaning of this word is using these examples and a dictionary.

42. NUISANCE

Here are two examples of possible use:
1. The new neighbor is becoming a nuisance, dropping in on us several times a day.
2. Folding up this map correctly is such a nuisance.

TREASURE BOX: Make mistakes.

Be flexible with the rules of grammar you have learned.
Do not try to be perfect in a day. Learn from your mistakes.

43. INDECISIVE

Here are two examples of potential use:
1. I can't stand his indecisive answers! I never know what's going on in his mind.
2. She didn't get this job, because she was so indecisive during the job interview.

Try to find what the meaning of this word is using these examples and a dictionary.

44. MATURE

Here are two examples of potential use:
1. He's only 15, but his mature approach to life is unbelievable.
2. When she left home to study in a foreign country she became more mature than I've ever expected.

Try to find the meaning of this word using these examples and a dictionary.

45. BUSY

Here are two examples of possible use:
1. Since he took up his new job, he's been extremely busy and has no time for friends and family.
2. Are we going to the cinema tonight? No, sorry, I'm busy. I have to finish this project for tomorrow.

I'm sure you'll know this word but try to check the meaning in a dictionary.

46. TO SPOT

Here are two examples of potential use:
1. He spotted me in the crowd at the concert.
2. Look at the two pictures and spot 14 differences between them.

Try to find the meaning of this word by using these examples and a dictionary.

47. TO EXAMINE

Here are two examples of potential use:
1. Every luggage will be examined at the airport.
2. Several doctors examined him thoroughly, but none of them found the cause of his migraines.

Try to find what the meaning of this word is by using these examples and a dictionary.

48. TO BLEED

Here are two examples of potential use:
1. I fell from the stairs and my leg was bleeding heavily.
2. Your hand is bleeding, what happened? I accidentally cut myself with a knife.

Try to find what the meaning of this word is by using these examples and a dictionary

49. TO BUMP INTO

Here are two examples of potential use:
1. What a surprise! I bumped into John when I was in Los Angeles.
2. I was fired, because I bumped into my boss in the pub, whereas I should have been ill in hospital.

Try to find what the meaning of this word is by using these examples and a dictionary.

TREASURE BOX: Cook your English.
{Yes you read it right, just like a chef, cook your own English, say it the way you feel it, make mistakes and learn.}

50. TO SNORE

Here are two examples of potential use:
1. I can't sleep at night, because my husband snores terribly.
2. We knew that he was already asleep, because we could hear him snoring.

Try to find the meaning of this word by using these examples.

REVIEW: 5

Choose the best word for the following definitions:

1. To observe carefully or critically.
   a. To Exchange
   b. To Examine
   c. To Consult

2. To hold steadfastly to; cherish.
   a. To Bump into
   b. To Estimate
   c. To Hug

3. Being in a state of putrefaction or decay; decomposed.
   a. Rotten
   b. Spot
   c. Nuisance

4. To plunge, especially headfirst, into water
   a. Dive
   b. Blink
   c. Examine

5. To use the nails or claws to dig or scrape at.
   a. To Suck
   b. To Bleed
   c. To Scratch

6. Of a higher nature or kind.
   a. Quality
   b. Superior
   c. Challenge

7. To expel air forcibly from the mouth and nose in an explosive action.
   a. To Sneeze
   b. To Spot
   c. To Snore

8. A space for storing goods.
   a. Storage
   b. Mature
   c. Superior

9. To emit or lose blood.
   a. To Suck
   b. To Bleed
   c. To Estimate

10. A call to engage in a contest, fight, or competition.
    a. To Suck
    b. To Challenge
    c. To Compete

51. TO SUCK

Here are two examples of potential use:
1. Don't suck so many sweets, or you'll have to go to the dentist!
2. The sleeping baby was sucking its thumb.

Try to find the meaning of this word by using these examples and a dictionary.

52. TO SNEEZE

Here are two examples of possible use:
1. I had to sell the cat, because it made me sneeze. I think I'm allergic to the fur.
2. You're sneezing all the time. Did you catch a cold?

Try to find the meaning of this word by using these examples and a dictionary

53. TO BLINK

Here are two examples of potential use:
1. He blinked when he came out into the light of the day.
2. Blink several times to get the lash out of your eye.

Try to find the meaning of this word by using these examples and a dictionary.

54. REFUND

Here are two examples of potential use:
1. I took the computer back to the shop and I was given a refund.
2. I was not satisfied with the journey, so the travel agency decided to give me 50% refund.

Try to find the meaning of this word by using these examples.

55. CHALLENGE

Here are two examples of potential use:
1. It was a very difficult task but she rose to the challenge.

2. Bribery is one of the biggest challenges that the government has to deal with.

Try to find what the meaning of this word is by using these examples and a dictionary.

56. DISCOUNT

Here are two examples of potential use:
1. If you buy more than one exemplar, you'll get a discount of 15%.
2. Polish railways offer 33% discount for students.

Try to find what the meaning of this word is by using these examples and a dictionary.

Treasure box:
{Remember that if you don't use these words you'll forget it in a short time. So please use them as much as possible.}

57. SUPERIOR

Here are two examples of potential use:
1. The worker was reported to his superiors for being frequently late for work.
2. I'm sure this marvelous painting is of a superior artist.

Try to find the meaning of this word by using these examples and a dictionary.

Now write your own sentences below.
1. _____
2. _____
3. _____

*Here is the answer to exercise 1

1. Fever.
   b. A rise in the temperature of the body; frequently a symptom of infection.

2. Economy.
   b. The system of production and distribution and consumption

3. Smoke.
   c. A cloud of fine particles suspended in a gas.

4. To survive.
   a. Continue to live through hardship or adversity.

5. Ill
   c. Not healthy or sick.

6. To burn.
   a. To undergo rapid combustion or consume fuel in such a way as to give off heat.

7. Technique.
   c. A practical method or art applied to some particular task.

8. Bridge.
   b. A structure that allows people or vehicles to cross an obstacle such as a river or canal or railway etc.

9. To cross.
   b. To intersect or meet at a point.

10. Sudden.
    c. Happening without warning or in a short space of time.

How many of these words can you remember and use now?

58. STORAGE

Here are two examples of potential use:
1. Our furniture will remain in the storage until we find a new house.
2. The goods are all in our storage and we are ready to send them to you if you buy them on the Internet.

Try to find the meaning of this word by using these examples and a dictionary.

59. DIVE

Here are two examples of potential use:
1. She made a graceful dive into the pool.
2. They are diving to find treasure from the Italian shipwreck.

Try to find the meaning of this word by using these examples and a dictionary.

60. TO SCRATCH

Here are two examples of potential use:
Ex 1.: I left my car near the forest and I found it in the morning with the roof scratched heavily by the falling branches.
Ex 2.: **He now has a very successful business but he started from scratch.**

Try to find the meaning of this word by using these examples and a dictionary.

REVIEW: 6

Fill in the gaps with the best answers.

1) Go to the _____ and try this dress on.
   [a] checkout
   [b] exchange
   [c] changing room

2) Look at the _____! This shirt is too expensive. You can't afford it.
   [a] price tag
   [b] size
   [c] shopping list

3) I've lost my _____ but I'd like to return this scarf. Is it possible?
   [a] afford
   [b] shopping list
   [c] receipt

4) I would like to return this electric kettle. Can I have a _____?
   [a] price tag
   [b] refund
   [c] checkout

5) May I try it on?—Yes, what _____ are you?
   [a] try on
   [b] size
   [c] shopper

6) I'd like to get a _____ for these shoes because they are too tight.
[a] refund
[b] size
[c] try on

7) There was a big sale at that mall last week. Many _____ arrived at 4 a.m. to ensure a good place in line.
[a] shopper
[b] shoppers
[c] fitting room

8) We go to the _____ because it sells products at lower prices.
[a] changingroom
[b] discountstore
[c] afford

9) Henry lost his _____ and forgot to buy pork loin.
[a] receipt
[b] refund
[c] shopping list

10) She worked on the _____ at the supermarket last summer.
[a] checkout
[b] discount store
[c] changing room

11) Have you got this dress in black?—Yes, we have.—Can I _____?
[a] try it on
[b] exchange
[c] refund

12) I missed my train because I was queuing at the
_____ in a supermarket.
[a] checkout
[b] size
[c] receipt

13) I bought this sweater yesterday but it's too small. Can I
_____ it please?
[a] checkout
[b] exchange
[c] receipt

14) We don't have enough money. We aren't able to
_____ such expensive shoes.
[a] exchange
[b] afford
[c] refund

15) Where can I try the jeans on?—The _____ is
over there.
[a] discount store
[b] fitting room
[c] price tag

16) This jacket _____ you very well. I think you
should buy it.
[a] suit
[b] suits
[c] sizes

17) This tailcoat was very expensive but Ted could still
_____ it.
[a] suit
[b] refund
[c] afford

18) You spend too much on clothes. Don't you look at the
_____ before buying something?
  [a] size
  [b] price tag
  [c] changing room

19) I'm going to buy her the blue dress. This color
_____ her best.
  [a] suits
  [b] tries on
  [c] refunds

20) If you don't like the color of the pullover, you can
_____ it. You'll get another one.
  [a] receipt
  [b] checkout
  [c] exchange

61. ROTTEN

Here are two examples of potential use:
1. A—What's that terrible stink? B—It's the rotten egg.
2. The weather was awful and our flight was delayed. It was a rotten journey.

Try to find the meaning of this word by using these examples and a dictionary.

62. TO ESTIMATE

Here are two examples of potential use:
1. I tried to estimate how far the town is, but it was difficult because the map was not very precise.

2. it's been estimated that less and less people are likely to live to be 100 years old.

Try to find the meaning of this word by using these examples and a dictionary.

63. ACCESSIBLE

Here are two examples of potential use:
1. The city is accessible only by boat or plane.
2. The book is not accessible for children below 12.

Try to find the meaning of this word by using these examples and a dictionary.

TREASURE BOX: Be loud!
What you may consider loud (especially for Japanese society) is just right for English language for people to hear and possibly understand you.

64. TO PRONOUNCE

Here are two examples of potential use:
1. Don't pronounce the letter "k" in the word "know".
2. Sorry, I didn't catch your name, could you pronounce it?

Try to find the meaning of this word by using these examples and a dictionary.

65. CONVENIENT

Here are two examples of potential use:
1. We may meet at any time convenient to you.

2. The room is very convenient because of all its useful electronic devices.

Try to find the meaning of this word by using these examples and a dictionary.

66. TO TRANSMIT

Here are two examples of potential use:
1. My favorite program wasn't transmitted yesterday because of bad weather conditions.
2. The disease transmitted incredibly fast, killing every person that was affected.

Try to find the meaning of this word by using these examples and a dictionary.

67. TROUBLESOME

Here are two examples of potential use:
1. I'm going to the dentist today with my troublesome tooth.
2. She has so many problems with her troublesome children.

Try to find the meaning of this word by using these examples and a dictionary.

68. "SUPERFICIAL"

Meaning:
Concerned only with what is obvious or complete or not deep.

Example:
a. They had a **superficial** knowledge/understanding of the topic.

b. The storm only caused *superficial* damage to the building.

c. Despite a *superficial* resemblance, the paintings are by two different artists.

Look it up in your dictionary for more understanding.

Here is the answer to exercise 2

Choose the best word for the following definitions:

1. A movement from one place to another.
   c. Cross

2. A warning or intimation of something.
   c. To notice

3. An expression of esteem, respect, affection, or admiration.
   a. Compliment

4. A person or thing that is unknown or with whom one is unacquainted.
   b. Stranger

5. **To** present as worthy of acceptance or trial.
   b. Recommend

6. To convey thoughts, opinions, or emotions orally.
   b. To speak up

7. To make known formally or officially.
   c. To declare

8. To give aid or support.
   N/A =No answer or Not applicable.
   To give aid or support = to assist.

9. Possessing great material wealth.
   c. Rich

10. Payment for labor or services to a worker, especially remuneration on an hourly daily, or weekly basis or by the piece.
    b. Wage

69. COLLABORATE

Here are two examples of potential use:
1. They are collaborating with Microsoft on the new software.
2. He was accused of collaborating with the enemy and was sentenced to death.

Try to find the meaning of this word by using these examples and a dictionary.

70. STROLL

Here are two examples of potential use:
1. I love strolling on the beach in the early morning. It's so relaxing.
2. Tourists stroll in the streets of holiday resorts the whole summer.

Try to find the meaning of this word by using these examples and a dictionary.

REVIEW WITH EXERCISE: 7

Choose the best word for the following definitions:

1. Easy to approach, reach, enter, speak with, or use.
   a. Troublesome
   b. Accessible
   c. Mature

2. To put into the mouth and draw upon
   a. To spot
   b. To stroll
   c. To suck

3. Lacking definition; vague or indistinct.
   a. Ordinary
   b. Busy
   c. Indecisive

4. To send from one person, thing, or place to another; convey.
   a. To sneeze
   b. To transmit
   c. To compete

5. Full of distress or affliction.
   a. Troublesome
   b. Challenge
   c. Accessible

6. Suited or favorable to one's comfort, purpose, or needs
   a. Collaborate
   b. Superior
   c. Convenient

7. To work together, especially in a joint intellectual effort.
   a. To Spot
   b. To collaborate
   c. To pronounce

8. Lower someone's spirits; make downhearted
   a. To collaborate
   b. To demoralize
   c. To transmit

9. To announce authoritatively or officially.
   a. To pronounce
   b. To evaluate
   c. To deposit

10. To go for a leisurely walk
    a. To Stroll
    b. To transmit
    c. To collaborate

71. TO DEMORALISE

Here are two examples of potential use:
1. **The company's inconsistent policy has demoralized the staff.**
2. **Japan has determined not to be demoralized by the earthquake.**

Try to find the meaning of this word by using these examples.

72. DISTINCTIVE

Here are two examples of potential use:
1. it's easy to recognize him from distance because of his distinctive way of walking.

2. I think I wouldn't recognize him on the street, he isn't a very distinctive person.

Try to find the meaning of this word by using these examples and a dictionary.

73. TO WITHDRAW MONEY

Here are two examples of potential use:
1. You may withdraw $300 from your account each day from cash dispensers.
2. Somebody had stolen my credit cards and I found out later that all my money was withdrawn from my accounts

Try to find the meaning of this word by using these examples and a dictionary.

Here are the answers to the **Review: 3 exercise.**

1. **H**aving a happy disposition; in good spirits.
    d. Cheerful

2. To seek advice or information.
    b. To consult

3. To manufacture or create economic goods and services.
    a. To produce

4. Not hypocritical or deceitful; open; genuine.
    c. Sincere

5. Free from showiness or ostentation; unpretentious
    c. Modest

6. Something useful that can be turned to commercial or other advantage
   a. Commodity.

7. To engage the services of (a person) for a fee.
   a. To hire

8. To put or set into, between, or among.
   c. To inset = To insert

9. Degree or grade of excellence.
   b. Quality

10. To bring down amount, or degree; diminish.
    d. To reduce

Here is the answer for exercise;4

1. An angry dispute; a disagreement marked by a temporary or permanent break in friendly relationship.
   c. Quarrel

2. To deduct a certain amount from a bill, charge, etc.
   c. To discount

3. To breathe during sleep with hoarse or harsh sounds.
   b. To snore

4. To look with winking or half-shut eyes.
   b. Blink

5. To actively and attentively engaged in work or a pastime.
   a. Busy

6. Something offensive or annoying to individuals or to the community.
   c. Nuisance

7. **P**lain or undistinguished.
   c. Ordinary

8. A complete in natural growth or development, as plant and animal forms.
   b. Mature

9. **A**n approximate judgment or calculation, as of the value, amount, time, size, or weight of something
   c. Estimate

10. To give back or restore, especially money.
    a. Refund

74. DEPOSIT

Here are two examples of potential use:
1. If you want to open an account, you need to pay at least $300 deposit into it.
2. I paid $10 as a deposit so that the shop assistant could keep the jacket for me until the next day.

Try to find the meaning of this word by using these examples and a dictionary.

75. TO ACCELERATE

Here are two examples of potential use:
1. The car accelerated to overtake the truck.
2. The country's annual inflation accelerated up to 3% in March.

Try to find the meaning of this word by using these examples and a dictionary.

76. LANDLORD

Here are two examples of potential use:
1. Our landlord has increased the rent, but promised to buy us new beds.
2. After the students had thrown a big party, the landlord broke the contract and ordered them to leave his flat in 3 days.

Try to find the meaning of this word by using these examples and a dictionary.

77. TENANT

Here are two examples of potential use:
1. The rents are getting bigger and the number of tenants is falling down.
2. Tenants are real victims of the economic recession because their payments are getting smaller, whereas their rents are not.

Try to find the meaning of this word by using these examples and a dictionary.

78. EVALUATION

Here are two examples of potential use:
1. The evaluation of the progress of the students is impossible, unless we have a feedback from their teacher.
2. The evaluation of this method may take place only with the help of volunteers who will try it.

Try to find the meaning of this word by using these examples and a dictionary.

Here is the answer for exercise 5.

1. To observe carefully or critically.
   b. To Examine

2. To hold steadfastly to; cherish.
   c. To Hug

3. Being in a state of putrefaction or decay; decomposed.
   a. Rotten

4. To plunge, especially headfirst, into water
   a. Dive

5. To use the nails or claws to dig or scrape at.
   c. To Scratch

6. Of a higher nature or kind.
   a. Quality

7. To expel air forcibly from the mouth and nose in an explosive action.
   a. To Sneeze

8. A space for storing goods.
   a. Storage

9. To emit or lose blood.
   b. To Bleed

10. A call to engage in a contest, fight, or competition.
    c. To Challenge.

79. INVOICE

Here are two examples of potential use:
1. Do you need an invoice? No thanks, just a receipt please.
2. We always ask for a collective invoice for office goods each month.

Try to find the meaning of this word by using these examples and a dictionary.

80. INTEREST RATE

Here are two examples of potential use:
1. High interest rates discourage people from taking loans.
2. The best advertisement for a bank is to offer low interest rates.

Try to find the meaning of this word with these examples and a dictionary.

REVIEW WITH THIS EXERCISE: 8

Choose either (a) or (b) for the following definitions:

1. Different in nature or quality
   a. Distinct
   b. Consult

2. An occupant or inhabitant of any place.
   a. Landlord
   b. Tenant

3. To cause faster or greater activity
   a. To accelerate
   b. To deposit

4. The opposite of landlady
   a. Landlord
   b. Tenant

5. An itemized bill for goods sold or services provided
   a. Interest rate
   b. Invoice

6. Subject to or under the authority of a superior
   a. Subordinate
   b. Superior

7. The oppisite of deposit.
   a. To Evaluate
   b. To withdraw

8. Uncertain, hazardous, or risky
   a. Interest rate
   b. Chancy

9. The items represented on a list, as a merchant's stock ofgoods.
   a. Inventory.
   b. Evaluation.

10. The act of pledging, or engaging oneself.
    a. Distinct
    b. Commitment

81. CHANCY

Here are two examples of potential use:
1. It was a chancy thing to do. You could have died!
2. The chancier the thing is, the more he enjoys it.

Try to find the meaning of this word with these examples and a dictionary.

82. SUBORDINATE

Here are two examples of potential use:
1. The boss always gives the routine paper work to his subordinates.
2. Subordinates are often treated badly by their superiors.

Try to find the meaning of this word with these examples and a dictionary.

83. INVENTORY

Here are two examples of potential use:
1. Two new chairs appeared on the inventory of our room in the dormitory.
2. Their inventory of used computer equipment is the best in the city.

Try to find the meaning of this word by using these examples and a dictionary.

84. COMMITMENT

Here are two examples of potential use:
1. He's well known for his commitment to right-wing politics.
2. I'm afraid she's got too much commitment this month to help you with your project.

Try to find the meaning of this word by using these examples and a dictionary.

Here is the answer to the Rview: 7 exercise.

1. **E**asy to approach, reach, enter, speak with, or use.
    a. Troublesome
    (b) Accessible
    c. Mature

2. To put into the mouth and draw upon
    a. To spot
    b. To stroll
    (c) To suck

3. Lacking definition; vague or indistinct.
    a. Ordinary

b. Busy

(c). Indecisive

4. To send from one person, thing, or place to another; convey.
   a. To sneeze
   (b). To transmit
   c. To compete

5. Full of distress or affliction.
   (a). Troublesome
   b. Challenge
   c. Accessible

6. Suited or favorable to one's comfort, purpose, or needs
   a. Collaborate
   b. Superior
   (c). Convenient

7. To work together, especially in a joint intellectual effort.
   a. To Spot
   (b). To collaborate
   c. To pronounce

8. Lower someone's spirits; make downhearted
   a. To collaborate
   (b). To demoralize
   c. To transmit

9. To announce authoritatively or officially.
   (a). To pronounce
   b. To evaluate
   c. To deposit

10. To go for a leisurely walk
    (a). To Stroll
    b. To transmit

c. To collaborate

Treasure box:
{You have to continually learning English if you really want to be fluent at it.}

85. APPLICATION

Here are two examples of potential use:
1. I've sent 10 applications for different jobs and haven't received any answer yet.
2. If you want to go to the USA, you'll have to fill in the application form for your visa first.

86. TO MAINTAIN

Here are two examples of potential use:
1. The top priority of out company is to maintain our high standards.
2. Large buildings are very costly to maintain.

Try to find the meaning of this word by using these examples and a dictionary.

87. MARKET SHARE

Here are two examples of potential use:
1. Google's market share has recently increased from 10% to 30%.
2. Nokia is still the leader with the market share of 25%.

Try to find the meaning of this word by using these examples and a dictionary.

88. EXPANSION

Here are two examples of potential use:
1. There has been rapid expansion of the electronics industry as a result of technical development.
2. The multinational companies' expansion is one of the reasons for globalization.

Try to find the meaning of this word by using these examples and your dictionary.

Here is the answer to the Review: 8 exercise

Choose either (a) or (b) for the following definitions:

1. Different in nature or quality
    (a). Distinct
    b. Consult

2. An occupant or inhabitant of any place.
    a. Landlord
    (b). Tenant

3. To cause faster or greater activity
    (a). To accelerate
    b. To deposit

4. The opposite of landlady
    (a). Landlord
    b. Tenant

5. An itemized bill for goods sold or services provided
    a. Interest rate
    (b). Invoice

6. Subject to or under the authority of a superior
   (a). Subordinate
   b. Superior

7. The opposite of deposit.
   a. To Evaluate
   (b). To withdraw

8. Uncertain, hazardous, or risky
   a. Interest rate
   (b). Chancy

9. The items represented on a list, as a merchant's stock of goods.
   (a). Inventory
   b. Evaluation

10. The act of pledging, or engaging oneself.
   a. Distinct
   (b). Commitment

89. TO NEGOTIATE

Here are two examples of potential use:
1. The government decided to negotiate with the nurses on strike.
2. We are negotiating a new contract with our overseas customer.

Try to find the meaning of this word by using these examples and a dictionary.

90. REFERENCES

Here are two examples of potential use:
1. ith good references, you have a big chance of getting your dream job.

2. Young people often start low but after they gain some experience and get references from previous employers, they move up and find better jobs.

Try to find the meaning of this word by using these examples and your dictionary.

REVIEW: 9

Review with this exercise.

Choose either (a) or (b) for the following definitions:

1. An increase, enlargement, or development, especially in the activities of a company.
   a. Accelerate
   b. Expansion

2. The specific percentage of total industry sales of a particular product achieved.
   a. Market share
   b. Interest rate

3. To arrange for or bring about by discussion and settlement of terms.
   a. To evaluate
   b. To negotiate

4. A verbal or written request, as for a job, etc
   a. Application
   b. Commitment

5. To keep in a specified, condition, state, position, etc.
   a. To transmit
   b. To maintain

91. REWARD

Here are two examples of potential use:
1. The police have promised a reward for revealing the hiding place of the murderer.
2. Our boss often gives rewards to employees who contribute to the company's success.

Try to find the meaning of this word by using these examples and a dictionary.

92. VACANCY

Here are two examples of potential use:
1. There are three vacancies for shop assistants in the new shopping mall.
2. I wonder if the vacancy for a secretary advertised last week is still on.

Try to find the meaning of this word by using these examples and a dictionary.

93. SUPPLEMENT

Here are two examples of potential use:
1. The money she earns from translating documents is just a supplement to her main income.
2. If you want to use the hotel swimming pool and sauna, you will have to pay a supplement to your accommodation.

Try to find the meaning of this word by using these examples and a dictionary.

Here is the answer to the exercise. 9

Choose either (a) or (b) for the following definitions:

1. An increase, enlargement, or development, especially in the activities of a company.
   a. Accelerate
   (b). Expansion

2. The specific percentage of total industry sales of a particular product achieved.
   (a). Market share
   b. Interest rate

3. To arrange for or bring about by discussion and settlement of terms.
   a. To evaluate
   (b). To negotiate

4. A verbal or written request, as for a job, etc
   (a). Application
   b. Commitment

5. To keep in a specified, condition, state, position, etc.
   a. To transmit
   (b). To maintain

94. INCAPABLE

Here are two examples of potential use:
1. The company seems incapable of protecting itself against the competition.
2. I think she's incapable of walking past a clothes shop without buying something.

Try to find the meaning of this word by using these examples and a dictionary.

REVIEW: 10

Review with this exercise.

Choose the either **a** or **b** that matches the following definitions;

1. A position, office, or place of accommodation that is unfilled or unoccupied
   a. Vacancy
   b. Application

2. Something given or received in recompense for worthy behavior
   a. Expansion
   b. Reward

3. Something added to complete a thing, make up for a deficiency
   a. Negotiate
   b. Supplement

4. Unable to perform adequately; incompetent
   a. Incapable
   b. Expansion

5. A statement about a person's qualifications, character, and dependability
   a. Application
   b. References

95. ESSENTIAL GOODS

Here are two examples of potential use:
1. The cost of essential goods is much higher in the west of Europe.

2. People are afraid that joining Euro zone would increase the cost of essential goods in Poland.

Try to find what the meaning of this word is using these examples and a dictionary.

96. DEMAND

Here are two examples of potential use:
1. There's little demand for luxury goods in this poor area.
2. Good engineers are always in great demand.

Try to find the meaning of this word by using these examples and a dictionary.

97. SALES REPRESENTATIVE

Here are two examples of potential use:
1. People are fed up with numerous calls from sales representatives trying to sell them something they don't really need.
2. He makes good impression and is really persuasive, as a great sales representative.

98. REVENUE

Here are two examples of potential use:
1. Companies' revenues have fallen considerably at the time of the economic crisis.
2. Taxes that we pay are most of the government's revenue.

Try to find the meaning of this word by using these examples and a dictionary.

Here is the answer to the Review 10

Choose the either **a** or **b** that matches the following definitions;

1. A position, office, or place of accommodation that is unfilled or unoccupied
   (a). Vacancy
   b. Application

2. Something given or received in recompense for worthy behavior
   a. Expansion
   (b). Reward

3. Something added to complete a thing, make up for a deficiency
   a. Negotiate
   (b). Supplement

4. Unable to perform adequately; incompetent
   (a). Incapable
   b. Expansion

5. A statement about a person's qualifications, character, and dependability
   a. Application
   (b). References

99. PERFORMANCE

Here are two examples of potential use:
1. Our employees are given rewards based on their performance at work.
2. **Experience generally improves performance.**

Try to find the meaning of this word by using these examples and a dictionary.

REVIEW: 11

{Review with this exercise}

Choose a or b word that matches the following definitions;

1. To require or need as just, urgent, etc.
   a. Demand
   b. Negotiate

2. The collective items or amounts of income of a person, a state, etc.
   a. Essential goods
   b. Revenue

3. A person or organization designated by a company to solicit business on its behalf in a specified territory or foreign country.
   a. Sales representative
   b. Essential goods

4. The execution or accomplishment of work, acts, feats, etc
   a. Performance
   b. Demand

5. Basic goods or products necessary for everyday life.
   a. Essential goods
   b. performance

100. SUPPLIER

Here are two examples of potential use:
1. AT&T is a leading supplier of mobile telephone services in the United States.
2. The building company signed an agreement with the new supplier of building materials.

Try to find the meaning of this word by using these examples and a dictionary.

101. PARTNERS

Meaning and examples:
1: someone's husband or wife or the person someone has relationship with.
* His *partner*, his wife of 20 years, was shocked to hear about his accident.

2: one of two or more people, businesses, etc., that work together or do business together
* They are *partners* in the real estate business. * Singapore's most important trading *partner* is Indonesia.

3: someone who participates in an activity or game with another person
*We were each assigned a *partner* for the project.

102. PARTNERSHIP

Meaning
1. the state of being partners
2. a relationship between partners

Here examples of potential use:

Ex 1.: Partners of a partnership have greater liability for the possible losses than shareholders of a corporation.

Ex 2.: We both used to run our own business activity, but last year we established partnership.

Ex 3. *Their marriage is a **partnership** that has remained strong despite family illness.

Try to find the meaning of this word by using these examples and a dictionary.

103. DONATE

Here are two examples of potential use:
1. Some anonymous group of businessmen donated a huge amount of money to the charity.
2. Nowadays, many companies donate money to environmental protection to create the image of environment-friendly businesses.

Try to find the meaning of this word by using these examples and a dictionary.

104 SAFETY

Here are two examples of potential use;
1; It's important to learn about safety before using power tools.
2; He always wore safety glasses when working with chemicals.

*Here is the answer to exercise 11.

Choose a or b word that matches the following definitions;

1. To require or need as just, urgent, etc.
   (a). Demand
   b. Negotiate

2. The collective items or amounts of income of a person, a state, etc.
   a. Essential goods
   (b). Revenue

3. A person or organization designated by a company to solicit business on its behalf in a specified territory or foreign country.
   (a). Sales representative
   b. Essential goods

4. The execution or accomplishment of work, acts, feats, etc
   (a). Performance
   b. Demand

5. Basic goods or products necessary for everyday life.
   (a). Essential goods
   b. performance

105: HAMMER

Here are examples for possible use,
1. "John, please get me my new **hammer** to nail these pieces of wood together."
2. The sound of the rain **hammering** the metal roof of our camper made sleeping nearly impossible.

Try to understand the meaning of this word using these examples and even more use in your dictionary

REVIEW: 12

Review with exercise

Here is an exercise to review some of the vocabularies we've learned.

Use the following words to fill the gaps;

DONATE, SAFETY, HAMMER, PARTNERSHIP, SUPPLIER

A big _____ of essential goods have formed _____ with some smaller ones to _____ goods and money to help the people affected in the recent earthquake and tsunami. They especially demanded a quicker steps to make sure that there is enough provision of _____ environment for all.

They also _____ on the quick control of the nuclear radiation and better alternative energy provision in the nearest future.

106. IMPLEMENT

Here are two examples of potential use:
1. The new regulations will be implemented next month.
2. The government has finally implemented the promised changes to the taxation of income.

Try to find the meaning of this word by using these examples and a dictionary.

107. FACE

Here are two examples of potential use
Ex 1; she looked so beautiful at her wedding, her face glowed with happiness.
Ex 2; You need to face your difficulties rather than to run away from them.

108. EAGER

Here are two examples of potential use,
EX 1. She had heard so much about the new school, she was very eager to start.
EX 2. He was eager to show his wife the gift he had bought her.

Try to find the meaning of this word by using these examples and a dictionary.

109. EAGLE

Here are two examples of potential use;
Ex 1.   It is amazing how far an eagle can see.
Ex 2.   We both love birds, but the eagle is my husband's favorite.

Try to find the meaning of this word by using these examples and a dictionary.

REVIEW: 12

Here is the answer to the exercise;

Use the following words to fill the gaps;

DONATE, SAFETY, HAMMER, PARTNERSHIP, SUPPLIER

A big _____ SUPPLIER _____ of essential goods have formed _____ PARTNERSHIP _____ with some smaller ones to _____ DONATE _____ goods and money to help the people affected in the recent earthquake and tsunami. They especially demanded a quicker step to make sure that there is enough provision of _____ SAFETY _____ environment for all.

They also _____ HAMMERED _____ on the quick control of the nuclear radiation and better alternativeenergy provision in the nearest future.

110: LOAFER

Here are two examples for possible uses;
1. He saved up his lawn-mowing money all summer to buy a pair of loafers.
2. I guess the boy turned out to be a loafer because his father was such a lazy guy.

111. GROCERY

Here are two examples of potential uses;

1. One of her favorite ways to spend the afternoon was shopping for groceries.
2. She has to eat something before she goes to the grocery store, or she will buy too much food!

REVIEW: 13

Here is an exercise to review

Fill in the gaps with the following list of words.

IMPLEMENT, FACE, EAGER, EAGLE, LOAF, GROCERY
1. "What this generation must do is _____ its problems" (John F. Kennedy).
2. He is disliked by almost everyone because he is a _____
3. The government have decided to _____ the new procedures.
4. She was very _____ to go back to school.
5. Like all birds of prey,_____ have very large hooked beaks for tearing flesh from their preys strong muscular legs, and powerful talons.
6. Cities everywhere are banning plastic _____ bags, while one lonely California lawyer fights for their survival.

112: MOBILITY

Here are two examples of potential use:
Ex 1.: People with families don't normally take up this job, because it involves permanent mobility.
Ex 2.: Some young people just cannot stay in one place too long. They often find jobs that require high mobility.

Try to find the meaning of this word by using these examples.

113: TO REMIND

Here are two examples of potential use:

Ex 1.: Remind me to call Sue in the evening, will you?

Ex 2.: I was enjoying myself at the party, when she had to remind me that I must get up early to work. So I left and went home angry.

Try to find the meaning of this word by using these examples and a dictionary.

114. TRAFFIC JAM

Here are two examples of potential use:

Ex 1.: I was late again, because I was stuck in a huge traffic jam for an hour. I shouldn't have gone by car during rush hours.

Ex 2.: The main road in the centre of the town has been closed recently causing terrible traffic jams.

You probably know this but, try to find the meaning by using these examples and a dictionary.

115. TO FORECAST

Here are two examples of potential use:

Ex 1.: The experts forecast a huge rise in unemployment due to the economic crisis.

Ex 2.: A lot of snow has been forecast for the following week.

Try to find the meaning of this word by using these examples and a dictionary.

Here is the answer to the exercise

REVIEW: 13

Fill in the gaps with the following list of words.

IMPLEMENT, FACE, EAGER, EAGLE, LOAF, GROCERY

1. "What this generation must do is _____ FACE _____ its problems" (John F. Kennedy).
2. He is disliked by almost everyone becase he is a _____ LOAFER _____
3. The government have desided to _____ IMPLEMENT _____ the new procedures.
4. She was very _____ EAGER _____ to go back to school.
5. Like all birds of prey,_____ EAGLES _____ have very large hooked beaks for tearing flesh from their preys strong muscular legs, and powerful talons.
6. Cities everywhere are banning plastic _____ GROCERY _____ bags, while one lonely California lawyer fights for their survival.

116: DURING

Here are two examples for potential uses;

EX 1. The restaurant is open **during** the day.
EX 2. The period **during** which he grew to adulthood.

Try to find the meaning by using these examples and a dictionary.

117.: WHILE

Here are two examples of potential use;

EX 1. hile she appreciated the honor, she could not accept the position.

EX 2. I stay inside while it's raining.

Try to find the meaning and different ways of using it through these examples and a dictionary.

118. LAKE

Here are two examples of potential use:

Ex 1.: The Lake District, a rural area in North West England, is famous for its beautiful lakes surrounded by mountains.

Ex 2.: We took a boat to cross the lake, whereas the others swam across it.

Try to find the meaning of this word by using these examples and a dictionary.

119. TO HAPPEN

Here are two examples of potential use:

Ex 1.: What will happen if your parents find out that you're here?

Ex 2.: What happened to you? You look terrible!

Try to find the meaning of this word by using these examples and a dictionary.

120: TO OFFER

Here are two examples of potential use:

Ex 1.:   Can I offer you a drink?

Ex 2.:   He offered that we go to the cinema tonight, but I refused.

Try to find the meaning of this word by using these examples and a dictionary.

121. RESPONSIBLE

Here are two examples of potential use:

Ex 1.:   I'm not afraid of lending him money or my car, because he's a very responsible person.

Ex 2.:   We're looking for a responsible babysitter to look after our daughter.

Try to find the meaning of this word by using these examples and a dictionary.

REVIEW: 14

Choose the best word that fits the following definitions.

TRAFFIC JAM, WHILE, DURING, REMIND, MOBILITY, FORECAST

1. The ability to move or be moved freely and easily.(MOBILITY)
2. In spite of the fact that or at the same time that someting else is happening.(WHILE)
3. A number of vehicles so obstructed that they can scarcely move. (TRAFFIC JAM)
4. To contrive or plan beforehand; prearrange.(FERECAST)
5. Throughout the course or duration of.(DURING)
6. To assist (somebody acting or reciting) by suggesting the next words of something forgotten or imperfectly learned. (REMIND)

122:LIBRARY

Here are two examples of potential use:
Ex 1.:   Ordinary students don't have money to buy new books, so they borrow them from a library.
Ex 2.:   When I'm bored, I go to the local library to borrow something interesting to read

Try to find the meaning by using these examples and a dictionary.

123:UNIT

Here are two examples of potential use:

Ex 1.: The standard unit of currency in Germany is the Euro.

Ex 2.: The book is divided into 12 units, each focused on different area of English grammar.

Try to find the meaning of this word by using these examples and a dictionary.

Here is an exercise to review our vocabularies.

REVIEW: 15

Use the correct form of the following words to fill in the gaps;

LAKE, HAPPEN, OFFER, RESPONSIBLE, UNIT, LIBRARY.

1. **The situation** _____ **us the opportunity to learn more.**
2. **The cabinet is** _____ **to the parliament.**
3. **There is a** _____ **of spilled coffee on my desk**
4. **If anything** _____ **to me it'll be your fault.**
5. **Degree centigrade is** a _____ of measurement for temperature.
6. **A** _____ **is a place in which literary and artistic materials, such as books, periodicals, newspapers can be borrowed.**

124: TO SUNRISE

Here are two examples of potential use:
Ex 1.:   She finished studying for her exam at sunrise.
Ex 2.:   We set off early at sunrise.

Try to find the meaning of this word by using these examples and a dictionary.

125:. TO PUSH

Here are two examples of potential use:
Ex 1.: He pushed her into the water, as he didn't know that she can't swim.

Ex 2.: They pushed the door open and went in making all the people look at them.

Try to find the meaning of this word by using these examples and a dictionay.

126. TO HURT

Here are two examples of potential use:
Ex 1.: He hurt his leg when he fell from the tree.
Ex 2.: She hurt him so much, when she left without a word of explanation.

Try to find the meaning of this word by using these examples and a dictionary.

127. LAW

Here are two examples of potential use:
Ex 1.:   You can't drink alcohol in the street according to the law.
Ex 2.:   They imposed a law that forbids smoking in restaurants.

Try to find the meaning of this word by using these examples and a dictionary.

Answer to review 15

Use the correct form of the following words to fill in the gaps;

LAKE, HAPPEN, OFFER, RESPONSIBLE, UNIT, LIBRARY.

1.   The situation _____ offered _____ us the opportunity to learn more.
2.   The cabinet is _____ responsible _____ to the parliament.

3. There is a _____ lake _____ of spilled coffee on my desk
4. If anything _____ happens _____ to me it'll be your fault.
5. Degree centigrade is a _____ unit _____ of measurement for temperature.
6. A _____ library _____ is a place in which literary and artistic materials, such as books, periodicals, newspapers can be borrowed.

128: FACTORY

Here are two examples of potential use:
Ex 1.: We visited the sweets factory and we had our stomachs full of chocolate.
Ex 2.: Nobody wants to live here because it's an area of factories, full of noise and smoke.

Try to find the meaning by using these examples and a dictionary.

129:. ENVIRONMENT

Here are two examples of potential use:
Ex 1.: Our natural environment is regularly threatened by oil spills and pollution.
Ex 2.: If you sort out rubbish, you help the environment.

Find the meaning of this word by using these examples and a dictionary.

REVIEW: 16

Here is an exercise to review our vocabularies.

Fill in the gaps with correct form of the following words;

SUNRISE, PUSH, LAW, HURT, ENVIRONMENT, FACTORY.

1. **The author** _____ **her latest book by making appearances in bookstores.**
2. **All citizens are equal before the** _____
3. **The scandal** _____ **the candidate's chances for victory.**
4. **We shall never understand the natural** _____ **until we see it as a living organism**
5. **Assembly line is a m**echanical system in a _____ whereby an article is conveyed through sites at which successive operations are performed on it.
6. We worked **from** _____ **to sunset.**

130: DAWN

Here are two examples of potential use:
Ex 1.: People from villages wake up at dawn and start working. I can't imagine living like that. I'd rather sleep until midday.
Ex 2.: When I was a child, I used to wake up at dawn and watch the sun rising.

Find the meaning of this word by using these examples and a dictionary.

Answer to review 16

SUNRISE, PUSH, LAW, HURT, ENVIRONMENT, FACTORY.

1. The author <u>pushed</u> her latest book by making appearances in bookstores.
2. All citizens are equal before the <u>law</u>
3. The scandal <u>hurt</u> the candidate's chances for victory.
4. We shall never understand the natural <u>environment</u> until we see it as a living organism
5. **Assembly line is a m**echanical system in a **<u>factory</u>** whereby an article is conveyed through sites at which successive operations are performed on it.
6. We worked from <u>sunrise</u> to sunset.

131:TO DISCUSS

Here are two examples of potential use:
Ex 1.:   We are meeting today to discuss our problems.
Ex 2.:   The book discusses English literature.

Fnd the meaning of this word by using these examples and a dictionary.

132. TO RECOGNIZE / RECOGNISE

Here are two examples of potential use:
Ex 1.: Have you seen Helen recently? She looks so different that I hardly recognized her!
Ex 2.: This is the castle that we visited ten years ago when you were a child. Do you recognize it?

Find the meaning of this word by using these examples and a dictionary.

133: FOREIGN

Here are two examples of potential use:
Ex 1.: He can speak two foreign languages: English and French.
Ex 2.: Remember to take your passport. The tour goes through four foreign countries.

Find the meaning of this word by using these examples and a dictionary.

134:CURRENTLY

Here are two examples of potential use:
Ex 1.: All the options are currently available. You can choose whatever you want.
Ex 2.: Your question is currently being discussed. You will get an answer in a short time.

Find the meaning of this word by using these examples and a dictionary.

135:JOBLESS

Here are two examples of potential use:
Ex 1.: The jobless may be given unemployment benefits for no longer than 12 months.
Ex 2.: She often threatens his jobless husband to leave him, unless he finds a job. He seems not to care.

Find the meaning of this word by using these examples and a dictionay.

REVIEW: 17

Here is an exercise for review

Fill in the gaps with an appropriate form of the following words;

DAWN, DISCUSS, RECOGNIZE, FOREIGN, CURRENTLY, JOBLESS.

1. That doesn't sound related, it sounds _____ to the present discussion.
2. Many of the _____ moved to town is causing more competition.
3. She is _____ working as a lab technician.
4. The union leaders are meeting to _____ about the fate of the factory.
5. They had decided to leave at _____ to be able to make their appointment.
6. The club's president _____ the new member.

136:BRIBE

Here are two examples of potential use:
Ex 1.: Our last boss was convicted for 5 years' imprisonment for accepting bribes.
Ex 2.: Doctors are believed to take bribes from drug companies.

Find the meaning of this word by using these examples and a dictionary.

137. REFRAIN

Here are two examples of potential use:

EX1. I usually **refrain** from singing in public, but when I do, I always sing the **refrain**.

EX2. I was going to make a joke but I *refrained myself from doing so.*

Find the meaning of this word by using these examples and a dictionary.

138. BORROWER (DEBTOR)

Here are two examples of potential use:

Ex 1.: The debtor is obliged to pay their financial obligation at the time mentioned in the agreement.

Ex 2.: The borrowers shall provide the history of financial statements and the information on their incomes, if they want to take the loan.

Find the meaning of this word by using these examples.

139. POLITE

Here are two examples of potential use:

Ex 1.: I know you don't like them, but you should be more **polite** to them anyway.

Ex 2.: Teachers complain that there are no **polite** pupils nowadays.

Find the meaning of this word by using these examples and a dictionary.

Answer to review 17

Fill in the gaps with an appropriate form of the following words;

DAWN, DISCUSS, RECOGNIZE, FOREIGN, CURRENTLY, JOBLESS.

1. That doesn't sound related, it sounds _____ **foreign** _____ to the present discussion.
2. Many of the _____ **jobless** _____ moved to town is causing more competition.
3. She is _____ **currently** _____ working as a lab technician.
4. The union leaders are meeting to _____ **discuss** _____ about the fate of the factory.
5. They had decided to leave at _____ **dawn** _____ to be able to make their appointment.
6. The club's president _____ **recognized** _____ the new member.

140. TICKET

Here are two examples of potential use:

Ex 1.: If you want to see the latest play in the theatre, you need to buy the **tickets** in advance. The play is very popular.

Ex 2.: I'm sorry, you don't have a **ticket**, Sir. You can not be allowed to get on board.

Find the meaning of this word by using these examples and a dictionary.

141. WARRANTY (GUARANTEE)

Here are two examples of potential use:

Ex 1.: The computer's on a 2-year **warranty**. Unfortunately, it broke down after the warranty had run off.

Ex 2.: There are manufacturers that give you a lifelong **guarantee** for their top-quality products.

Find the meaning of this word by using these examples and a dictionary.

REVIEW: 18

Here is an exercise to review our vocabularies.

Fill in the gaps with the right forms of the following words;

BRIBE, REFRAIN, DEBTOR, POLITE, TICKET, WARRANTY

1. If a creditor has loaned money, performed services or provided a _____ with a product, that _____ has to pay the creditor.
2. You are asked to _____ from smoking, drinking (alcohol) and eating in this hall.
3. The stereo and the refrigerator came with a three-year _____ but one year for the TV.
4. We bought _____ for the opera I got one for over speeding on the way there.
5. She received some _____ applause despite the mistakes in her performance.

142. PATIENCE

Here are two examples of potential use:
Ex 1.: I don't have the **patience** to wait in line for hours just to buy a ticket.
Ex 2.: Investors need to have **patience**. The economy will improve soon.

Find the meaning of this word by using these examples and dictionary.

143. T V COMMERCIAL

Here are two examples of potential use:

Ex 1.: I don't watch films on TV because of the annoying **TV commercials** every 20 minutes.

Ex 2.: Billboards and other outdoor advertising have become more popular and cheaper than **TV commercials.**

Find the meaning of this word by using these examples and a dictionary.

144. WARDROBE

Here are two examples of potential use:

Ex 1.: You buy too many clothes. Your **wardrobe** is too small for it.

Ex 2.: I decided to change my summer **wardrobe**, because all my clothes are so monotonous.

Find the meaning of this word by using these examples and a dictionary.

145. ENORMOUS

Here are two examples of potential use:

Ex 1.: Have you ever seen such an **enormous** house? It must have at least 200 rooms.

Ex 2.: This film was an **enormous** success and earned $ 1.000.000 in one week.

Find the meaning of this word by using these examples and a dictionary.

Answer to REVIEW: 18

Fill in the gaps with the right forms of the following words;

BRIBE, REFRAIN, DEBTOR, POLITE, TICKET, WARRANTY

1. If a creditor has loaned money, performed services or provided a _____ **debtor** _____ with a product, that _____ **debtor**_____ has to pay the creditor.
2. You are asked to _____ **refrain** _____ from smoking, drinking (alcohol) and eating in this hall.
3. The stereo and the refrigerator came with a three-year _____ **warranty** _____ but one year for the TV.
4. We bought _____ **ticket** _____ for the opera I got one for over speeding on the way there.
5. She received some _____ **polite** _____applause despite the mistakes in her performance.

146. TO SMELL

Here are two examples of potential use:
Ex 1.: The milk is not fresh. Can you **smell** it?
Ex 2.: He got a cold and couldn't **smell** very well.

Find the meaning of this word by using these examples and a dictionary.

147. PEACE

Here are two examples of potential use:
Ex 1.: All I want is to have some **peace** after the stressful day.
Ex 2.: Terrorism is a serious problem that threatens world **peace**.

Find the meaning of this word by using these examples and a dictionary.

REVIEW: 19

Here is the review of some vocabularies.

Fill in the gaps with the correct form of the following words;

PATIENCE, WARDROBE, ENORMOUS, SMELL, BRIBE, PEACE, TV COMMERCIAL.

1. We chose not to undertake the project because of the _____ costs involved.
2. I can't _____ anything because I'm so stuffed up.
3. After many years of war, people on both sides were longing for _____
4. I offered the children a _____ for finishing their homework.
5. She has a new summer _____ and she almost can't wait for summer to come.
6. The average American sees and hears thousands of _____messages each day.
7. She treated her students with great _____ and humor.

148. TEAR

Here are two examples of potential use:
Ex 1.: I saw **tears** streaming down her face. She was not sad they were **tears** of joy.
Ex 2.: My mum couldn't hide her **tears** when she saw me in a white wedding dress.

Try to find the meaning of this word by using these examples and a dictionary.

149. RAINBOW

Here are two examples of potential use:

Ex 1.: The **rainbow** is a symbol of the alliance with God.

Ex 2.: I've never seen such a beautiful **rainbow** with all seven saturated colours extending from the heavy clouds to the ground.

Try to find the meaning of this word by using these examples and a dictionary.

150. TO HIT

Here are two examples of potential use:

Ex 1.: She **hit** the thief hard on the stomach with her bag.

Ex 2.: The ball **hit** the ground and the match was over.

Try to find the meaning of this word by using these examples and a dictionary.

Treasure box: Explain your vocabulary.

When you are stuck and you cannot remember the vocabulary you want to use, simply explain it then you or the person you are talking to may remember or catch what you intend to say.

151. PENSION

Here are two examples of potential use:

Ex 1.: Older people often find it hard to live on their **pensions** only.

Ex 2.: I'd like to draw my **pension** much earlier. I'm really fed up with my job.

Try to look up the meaning of this word in the dictionary and make more examples.

Answer to Review: 19

Here is the answer to the exercise.

Fill in the gaps with the correct form of the following words;

PATIENCE, WARDROBE, ENORMOUS, SMELL, BRIBE, PEACE, TV COMMERCIAL.

1. We chose not to undertake the project because of the _____ **enormous** _____ costs involved.
2. I can't _____ **smell** _____ anything because I'm so stuffed up.
3. After many years of war, people on both sides were longing for _____ **peace** _____
4. I offered the children a _____ **bribe** _____ for finishing their homework.
5. She has a new summer _____ **wardrobe** _____ and she almost can't wait for summer to come.
6. The average American sees and hears thousands of _____ **tv commercial** _____ messages each day.
7. She treated her students with great _____ **patience** _____ and humor.

How many did you get right?

152. CRIME

Here are two examples of potential use:
Ex 1.: He was sentenced to prison for having committed a terrible **crime.**
Ex 2.: Those who sell drugs commit a serious **crime.**

Try to understand the meaning of this word through these examples and a dictionary.

153. FOCUS

Here are two examples of potential use;
EX 1. We need to *focus* our efforts on getting the work done.
EX 2. She has an amazing ability to *focus* for hours at a time.

Try to find the meaning of this word using these examples and even more uses in the dictionary.

REVIEW: 20

Here is an exercise to review our vocabularies and more.

Fill in the gaps with the right form of the following words.

TEAR, RAINBOW, PENSION, FOCUS, CRIME, HIT, MAKE, LET

1. They _____ off when they found a younger man for the job.
2. There are fairy tales of searches for the pot of gold at the foot of the _____
3. There's no greater _____ than forgetting your anniversary.
4. The day's news coverage _____ primarily/mainly *on* the scandal.
5. He was in _____ over the death of his dog.
6. The teacher _____ her students memorize long lists of vocabularies.
7. A break in the cloud _____ us see the top of the mountain.
8. The plate shattered when it _____ the floor.

154. ATTRACTIVE

Here are two examples of possible use;
EX 1. An *attractive* woman greeted us at the door.
EX 2. The camera has many **attractive** features at a very *attractive* price.

Find the meaning of the word using a dictionary and try to make your sentences with it.

155. INCIDENT

Here are two examples of potential use;
EX 1. Two people were shot yesterday in two separate *incidents*.
EX 2. Many of such *incidents* go unreported.

Find the meaning of the word using these examples and a dictionary.

156. AVOID

Here are two examples of potential use;
EX 1. They successfully *avoided* each other for days.
EX 2. We need to *avoid* further delays.

Try to find the meaning of the word through these examples and a dictionary.

157. MEANINGFUL

Here are two examples of potential use;
EX 1. The test did not produce any *meaningful* results.
EX 2. He wanted to feel that his job was *meaningful*.

Find the meaning of the word using these examples and a dictionary.

REVIEW: 20

Here is the answer to the exercise to review our vocabularies.

Fill in the gaps with the right form of the following words.

TEAR, RAINBOW, PENSION, FOCUS, CRIME, HIT, MAKE, LET

1. They _____ **pensioned** him _____ off when they found a younger man for the job.
2. There are fairy tales of searches for the pot of gold at the foot of the _____ **rainbow** _____
3. There's no greater _____ **crime** _____ than forgetting your anniversary.
4. The day's news coverage _____ **focused** _____ primarily/mainly *on* the scandal.
5. He was in _____ **tears** _____ over the death of his dog.
6. The teacher _____ **made** _____ her students memorize long lists of vocabularies.
7. A break in the cloud _____ **let** _____ us see the top of the mountain.
8. The plate shattered when it _____ **hit** _____ the floor.

158. POTENTIAL

Here are two example of possible use;
EX 1. Doctors are excited about the new drug's **potential** benefits.
EX 2. He is a *potential* candidate for president.

Find the meaning of this word using these examples and a dictionary.

159. PROMOTE

Here are two examples of potential use;
1.   He was *promoted* to senior editor.
2.   Good soil *promotes* plant growth.

Try to find more meanings and uses of this word in the dictionary.

REVIEW: 21

Here is another exercise to review our vocabularies.

Fill in the gaps with the correct form of the following words.

ATTRACTIVE, INCIDENT, AVOID, MEANINGFUL, POTENTIAL, PROMOTE,

1. How can I _____ paying too much tax?
2. His ideas are _____ *to* many people.
3. The project has _____ risks and advantages.
4. The trip turned out to be very _____ to both of them.
5. Aside from a few isolated _____ the crowd was well-behaved.
6. The Chiba prefecture office distributed pamphlets _____ good dental hygiene.

160. GRUMBLE

Here are two examples of potential use;
1. There's been a lot of ***grumbling*** among the employees.
2. We could hear thunder ***grumbling*** in the distance.

Try to find the meaning of this word and more uses in the dictionay.

161. PROHIBIT

Here are two examples of potential use;
1. The rules of the company prohibit dating a coworker.
2. The prison's electric fence prohibits escape of the prisoners.

Find the meaning and more uses of the word in the dictionary.

162. CAMP

Here are two examples of potential use;
1. The children have fond memories of their last *summer camp*.
2. Our star pitcher injured his arm during the spring *camp* training.

Find the meaning of this word using the examples and a dictionary.

163. DESTINATION

Here are two examples of potential use;
1. After stopping for lunch, we continued on toward our **destination**.
2. The package arrived its **destination** two days later.

Try to find the meaning of this word using these examples and your dictionary.

REVIEW: 21

Here is the answer to the exercise. Fill in the gaps with the correct form of the following words.

ATTRACTIVE, INCIDENT, AVOID, MEANINGFUL, POTENTIAL, PROMOTE,

1. How can I ____ **avoid** ____ paying too much tax?
2. His ideas are ____ **attractive** ____ to many people.
3. The project has ____ **potential** ____ risks and advantages.
4. The trip turned out to be very ____ **meaningful** ____ to both of them.
5. Aside from a few isolated ____ **incident** ____ the crowd was well-behaved.
6. The Chiba prefecture office distributed pamphlets ____ **promoting** ____ good dental hygiene.

164. DISEMBARK

Here are two potential use;
1. **Several passengers disembarked** from the plane.
2. We will **disembark** the passengers at Yokohama shore.

Try to understand the meaning of this word and find more uses in the dictionary.

165. EMBARK (EMBARKMENT)

Here are two examples of potential use;
1. The troops are waiting to **embark** to IRAQ for a special mission.
2. He **embarked** on a new career because he wanted something more exciting.

Try to find the meaning of the word through these examples and a dictionary.

Treasure box: laugh at yourself.
When you make mistakes, laugh and joke about it. Do not worry it's all part of learning.

REVIEW: 22

Here is an exercise to review our vocabularies.

SECTION A; Match the following definitions with the words below.

GRUMBLE, PROHIBIT, CAMP, DESTNATION, DISEMBARK, EMBARK

1. To go on board a vehicle for transportation.
2. To complain quietly about something **or** to talk in an unhappy way.
3. A place to which one is journeying or to which something is sent.
4. To start or engage, enlist, or invest in an enterprise.
5. A group of people who support or believe in certain ideas.
6. To prevent or to forbid by authorityfrom doing something.
7. A place where athletes train before the beginning of a season.
8. To get out of a vehicle or craft.
9. A place usually in the mountains or by a lake where young people can do different activities during the summer.
10. To go or to remove ashore out of a ship.

166. CRISIS

Here are two examples of potential use;
1. Most people blame the government for the country's worsening economic *crisis.*
2. In times of national *crisis,* we need strong leaders we can trust.

Try to find the meaning and more uses in your dictionary.

167. DESTINY

Here are two examples of potential use;
1. They believed it was their **destiny** to be together.
2. The factory's closing shaped the **destiny** of the entire town.

Find the meaning to the word and a similar word in the dictionary.

168. GLOBAL

Here are two examples of potential use;
1. English is becoming a **global** language.
2. The **global** economy has become increasingly unstable.

Try to find the meaning of this word and more uses in the dictionary.

169. FATIGUE

Here are two examples of potential use;
1. We were overcome by **fatigue** after the long journey.
2. The drug's side effects include headache and *fatigue*.

Find the meaning by using these examples and your dictionary.

{**TREASURE BOX:**Try to use your English by;
a) reading out loud.
b) speaking to yourself in English when you're alone, it helps.}

REVIEW: 23

Here is the answer to the exercise to review our vocabularies.

Match the following definitions with the words below.

GRUMBLE, PROHIBIT, CAMP, DESTNATION, DISEMBARK, EMBARK

1. To go on board a vehicle for transportation. **EMBARK**
2. To complain quietly about something **or** to talk in an unhappy way. **GRUMBLE**
3. A place to which one is journeying or to which something is sent. **DESTINATION**
4. To start or engage, enlist, or invest in an enterprise. **EMBARK**
5. A group of people who support or believe in certain ideas. **CAMP**
6. To prevent or to forbid by authorityfrom doing something. **PROHIBIT**
7. A place where athletes train before the beginning of a season. **CAMP**
8. To get out of a vehicle or craft. **DISEMBARK**
9. A place usually in the mountains or by a lake where young people can do different activities during the summer. **CAMP**
10. To go or to remove ashore out of a ship. **DISEMBARK**

How many did you get right?

170. DEMONSTRATE

Here are two examples of potential use;
1. One of the instructors gave or did a *demonstration* of how to prune a tree.
2. Students took part in several peaceful *demonstrations* against the government.

Find the meaning in your dictionary and try to make your own sentences.

171. AGGRESSIVE

Here are two examples of potential use;
1. He started to get *aggressive* and began to shout.
2. The city began an *aggressive* campaign to encourage recycling.

Look up the meaning in your dictionary and practice making more sentences.

REVIEW: 24

Here is an exersice to review our vocabularies.

Fill in the gaps with the correct form of the following words.

DESTINY, CRISIS, GLOBAL, FATIGUE, DEMONSTRATE, AGGRESSIVE

1. A year ago, both companies were in _____ but revived by government's a**id.**
2. "I'm so _____ of your mother and her complaints about my food"
3. The company took _____ steps to prevent illegal use of their equipment.
4. The program allows users to do _____ searches through all the available data.
5. They brought some bread to share as a _____ of goodwill.
6. Nancy wondered whether it was her _____ to live in England and marry Melvyn.

172. ENCOURAGE

Here are two examples of potential use;
1. I am **encouraged** that the project seems to be moving ahead.
2. The program is meant to **encourage** energy savings.

Find the meaning in your dictionary and try to make more sentences.

173. ALTERNATIVE

Here are two examples of potential use;
1. We should have *alternative* [other] plans in case the weather is bad.
2. We could meet at the library or, *alternatively*, we could all meet at my house.

Look up the meaning in your dictionary and try to make your own sentences.

174. POOR

Here are two examples of potential use:
Ex 1.: It's a very **poor** country. Hardly can anyone afford a car there.
Ex 2.: They were too **poor** to afford even a pair of new shoes, whereas their children were living in a luxury.

Try to find the meaning of this word by using these examples and your dictionary.

175. STRAIGHTFORWARD

Here are two examples of potential use:
Ex 1; Using the computer program is fairly *straightforward*.
Ex 2; She gave a *straightforward* account of what happened.

Try to find the meaning of this word by using these examples and your dictionary.

Answers to review.23

Here is the answer to the exercise to review our vocabularies.

Fill in the gaps with the correct form of the following words.

DESTINY, CRISIS, GLOBAL, FATIGUE, DEMONSTRATE, AGGRESSIVE

1. A year ago, both companies were in ____ **crisis** ____ but revived by government's aid.
2. "I'm so ____ **fatigued** ____ of your mother and her complaints about my food"
3. The company took ____ **aggressive** ____ steps to prevent illegal use of their equipment.
4. The program allows users to do ____ **global** ____ searches through all the available data.
5. They brought some bread to share as a ____ **demonstration** ____ of goodwill.
6. Nancy wondered whether it was her ____ **destiny** ____ to live in England and marry Melvyn.

How many did you get right?

176. REMARKABLE

Here are two examples of potential use.
1. Competing in the Olympics is a *remarkable* achievement.
2. The girl has a *remarkable* talent.

Look the meaning up in the dictionary and make more sentences.

177. TERMINATE

Here are two examples of potential use:
Ex 1; The rail line **terminates** in Boston.
Ex 2; His contract was **terminated** last month.

Try to find the meaning of this word by using these examples and your dictionary.

REVIEW: 25

Here is an exercise to review our vocabularies.

Match the following definitions with the words below.

ENCOURAGE, ALTERNATE, REMARKABLE, TERMINATE, POOR, STRAIGHTFORWARD

1. lacking a normal or adequate supply of something specified.
2. Easy to do or understand : not complicated: honest and open.
3. To end in a particular way or at a particular place.
4. To make (someone) more determined, hopeful, or confident.
5. Existing or functioning outside of the established society: offering or expressing a choice.
6. Unusual or surprising : likely to be noticed.

178. HUMBLE

Here are two examples of possible use;
1. He is very *humble* about his achievements.
2. In my *humble* opinion [=in my opinion], he is the most talented actor on the stage today.

Look up the meaning of the word in the dictionary and make your own.

179. LEGACY

Here are two examples of potential use:

Ex 1.   She left us a *legacy* of a million dollars.

Ex 2.   The war left a **legacy** *of* pain and suffering.

Try to find the meaning of this word by using these examples and your dictionary.

180. RETAIN

Here are two examples of potential use:

1.   The TV show has **retained** its popularity for many years.

2.   The company's goal is to attract and **retain** good employees.

Try to find the meaning of this word by using these examples and your dictionary.

Treasure box: Gesture a lot with your head, face, hands and even your whole body when you speak. People will find you interesting and want to understand you by all means.

181. CONTEXT

Here are two examples of potential use:

Ex 1.   To really know a word, you must be able to use it *in context*. [=in a sentence with other words]

Ex 2.   The actor claimed he'd been quoted *out of context*.

Try to find the meaning of this word by using these examples and your dictionary.

REVIEW: 26

Here is the answer to the exercise.

Match the following definitions with the words below.

ENCOURAGE, ALTERNATE, REMARKABLE, TERMINATE, POOR, STRAIGHTFORWARD

1. lacking a normal or adequate supply of something specified. **POOR**
2. Easy to do or understand: not complicated: honest and open. **STRAIGHTFORWARD**
3. To end in a particular way or at a particular place. **TERMINATE**
4. To make (someone) more determined, hopeful, or confident. **ENCOURAGE**
5. Existing or functioning outside of the established society: offering or expressing a choice. **ALTERNATE**
6. Unusual or surprising: likely to be noticed. **REMARKABLE**

How many did you get right?

182. RALLY

Here are examples of possible use:
EX.1. Supporters held a *rally* for the candidate.
EX.2. The team's late-game *rally* [=*comeback*] helped them win the game.

Look up the meaning and make more sentences.

183. FRUSTRATE

Here are two examples of potential use:

Ex 1. It *frustrated* him to miss so many games because of injuries.

Ex 2. The lack of investors has *frustrated* them in their efforts to expand the company

Try to find the meaning of this word by using these examples and your dictionary.

REVIEW: 27

Here is the review of our vocabularies.

Fill the gaps with the correct form of the following words;

HUMBLE, LEGACY, RETAIN, CONTEXT, RALLY, FRUSTRATE.

1. A landlord may _____ part of your deposit if you break the lease.
2. She's not ashamed of her _____ beginnings.
3. The plans to rebuild Fukushime have been _____ by bureaucratic delays.
4. The home team _____ in the ninth inning to win the game.
5. The book puts these events in their proper historical and social _____
6. He left his children a _____ of love and respect.

184. TREMENDOUS

Here are two examples of potential use:
Ex 1. He has a *tremendous* amount of energy.
Ex 2. We had a *tremendous* time.

Try to find the meaning of this word by using these examples and your dictionary.

185. COMMENTARY

Here are two examples of potential use;
1. The magazine includes humor and social *commentary.*
2. He provided *commentary* during the game.

Try to find the meaning of this word and more uses in the dictionary.

Have a great day and happy English learning!

186. OVERTAKE

Here are two examples of potential use;
1. She *overtook* the other runners and went on to win the race.
2. The pounding rainstorm **overtook** them just outside the city.

Try to find the meaning of this word and more uses in the dictionary.

187. DISPLAY

Here are two examples of potential use;
1. Students *displayed* their projects at the science fair.
2. He *displayed* no emotion when I told him the news.

Try to find the meaning of this word and more uses in the dictionary.

Here is the answer to the review;25

Fill the gaps with the correct form of the following words;

HUMBLE, LEGACY, RETAIN, CONTEXT, RALLY, FRUSTRATE.

1. A landlord may ____ **retain** ____ part of your deposit if you break the lease.
2. She's not ashamed of her ____ **humble** ____ beginnings.
3. The plans to rebuild Fukushima have been ____ **frustrated** ____ by bureaucratic delays.
4. The home team ____ **rallied** ____ in the ninth inning to win the game.
5. The book puts these events in their proper historical and social ____ **context** ____
6. He left his children a ____ **legacy** ____ of love and respect.

How many did you get right?

188. MODE

Here are two examples of potential use;
1. We're changing the factory's *mode* [=method] of operation in order to save money.
2. When taking pictures indoors, put the camera in flash **mode**.

Find the meaning by using these examples and a dictionary.

189. HARDSHIP

Here are two examples of potential use;
1. He had suffered through considerable **hardship**.
2. The city has been experiencing a period of financial **hardship**.

Try to find the meaning of this word and more uses in the dictionary.

REVIEW: 26

Let's review our vocabularies with this exercise.

Macth the following definitions with the appropriate words bellow.

TREMENDOUS, COMMENTARY, OVERTAKE, DISPLAY, MODE, HARDSHIP.

1. A specified way of thinking, feeling, acting or doing something.
2. Very good or excellent : wonderful or very large or great.
3. To put (something) where people can see it or to show that you have (an emotion, quality, skill etc.
4. A spoken description of an event (such as a sports contest) as it is happening.
5. pain and suffering or something that causes pain, suffering, or loss.
6. To catch up with; draw even or level with or to pass after catching up with.

190. NEEDY

Here are two examples of potential use;
1. As a child, she was extremely *needy* and had no self-confidence.
2. Our church collected food for **the needy** last week.

Try to find the meaning of this word and more uses in the dictionary.

191. PERSONNEL

Here are two examples of potential use;
1. They've reduced the number of ***personnel*** working on the project.
2. Talk to ***personnel*** if you have any questions about your health insurance.

Try to find the meaning of this word and more uses in the dictionary.

192. PROLONG

Here are two examples of potential use;
1. Chemotherapy helped to ***prolong*** [=*extend*] her life.
2. Additives are used to **prolong** the shelf life of packaged food

Try to find the meaning of this word and more uses in the dictionary.

193. SOUR

Here are two examples of potential use;
1. The milk had turned/gone **sour.**
2. Their relationship ended *on a **sour** note.* [=ended unpleasantly]

Try to find the meaning of this word and more uses in the dictionary.

REVIEW: 26

Let's review our exercise

Macth the following definitions with the appropriate words bellow.

TREMENDOUS, COMMENTARY, OVERTAKE, DISPLAY, MODE, HARDSHIP.

1. A specified way of thinking, feeling, acting or doing something. **MODE**
2. Very good or excellent : wonderful or very large or great. **TRMENDOUS**
3. To put (something) where people can see it or to show that you have (an emotion, quality, skill etc. **DISPLAY**
4. A spoken description of an event (such as a sports contest) as it is happening. **COMMENTARY**
5. pain and suffering or something that causes pain, suffering, or loss. **HARDSHIP**
6. To catch up with; draw even or level with or to pass after catching up with. **OVERTAKE**

How many did you get right?

194. ASTONISH

These are two examples of possible use;
1. Her easy humor and keen intellect **astonishes** me.
2. The garden *astonishes* [=*amazes*] anyone who sees it.

Treasure box: You can also practice *speaking to yourself* in English, but be careful! Do this in your house or in your head, not when you are in the midst of people.

195. NOSEDIVE

Here are two examples of potential use;
1. The plane went *into a* **nosedive**.
2. The stock market took a *nosedive*.

Try to find the meaning of this word and more uses in the dictionary.

REVIEW: 27

Let's review our vocabularies with this exercise.

Fill in the gaps with the following words.

NEEDY, PERSONNEL, PROLONG, SOUR, ASTONISH, NOSEDIVE

1. He was too _____ to speak when he saw the present from his children.
2. The team's victory was _____ by an injury to one of their best players.
3. Generous people regularly give money and donate clothes to help the _____.
4. High interest rates are _____ the economy recession.
5. Everyone screamed as the plane suddenly went into a _____.
6. They've reduced the number of _____ working on the project.

196. FRAGILE

Here are two examples of potential use;
1. He is in an emotionally *fragile* state.
2. The two countries have formed a *fragile* coalition.

Try to find the meaning of this word and more uses in the dictionary.

197. CONFISICATE

Here are two examples of potential use;
1. Guards **confiscated** knives and other weapons from the prisoners.
2. The teacher **confiscated** all cell phones for the duration of the field trip.

Try to find the meaning of this word and more uses in the dictionary.

197. DISREGARD

Here are two examples of potential use;
1. Please *disregard* what I said before.
2. He *disregarded* his father's advice and left school.

Try to find the meaning of this word and more uses in the dictionary.

198. NARRATIVE

Here are two examples of potential use;
1. He is writing a detailed *narrative* of his life on the island.
2. People have questioned the accuracy of his *narrative*.

Try to find the meaning of this word and more uses in the dictionary.

REVIEW: 27

Let's review our vocabularies exercise.

SECTION A

Fill the gaps with the following words.

NEEDY, PERSONNEL, PROLONG, SOUR, ASTONISH, NOSEDIVE

1. He was too astonished to speak when he saw the present from his children.
2. The team's victory was **soured** by an injury to one of their best players.
3. Generous people regularly give money and donate clothes to help the **needy**.
4. High interest rates are **prolonging** the economy recession.
5. Everyone screamed as the plane suddenly went into a **nosedived**.
6. They've reduced the number of **personnel** working on the project.

How many did you get right?

199. FAMINE

Here are two possible use;
1. The *famine* affected half the country.
2. Millions were killed by war, drought, and *famine.*

Try to find the meaning using these examples and a dictionary.

200. OBSESS

Here are two examples of potential use;
1. She became more and more **obsessed** with the project.
2. I'm trying to **obsess** less about my weight.

Try to find the meaning of this word and more uses in the dictionary.

REVIEW: 28

Try this exersice to review some of the words that you have learned.

Choose the best word for the following definitions:

1. Possible to be easily broken or damaged.
   a. Fever
   b. To notice
   c. Fragile

2. To seize temporarily or permanently as way of penalty for use.
   a. Technique
   b. Confiscate
   c. To notice

3. To ignore (something) or treat (something) as unimportant.
   a. Compliment
   b. Disregard
   c. To recommend

4. A situation in which many people do not have enough food to eat.
   a. Famine
   b. Stranger
   c. Economy

5. To think about something unceasingly or persistently.
   a. Rich
   b. Recommend
   c. Obsess

6. A story that is told or written.
   a. Narrative
   b. To speak up
   c. To notice

201. REMOTE

Here are two examples of potential use;
1. The mission is to transport medical supplies to **remote** areas of the globe.
2. There is a **remote** possibility that I'll be free Friday night.

Try to find the meaning of this word and more uses in the dictionary.

202. INVOLVE

Here are two examples of potential use:
Ex 1. She remained **involved with** the organization for many years.
Ex 2. Renovating the house **involved** hiring a contractor.

Try to find the meaning of this word by using these examples and your dictionary.

203. FACILITATE

Here are two examples of potential use:
Ex 1. Cutting taxes may **facilitate** economic recovery.
Ex 2. Her rise to power was **facilitated** by her influential friends.

Try to find the meaning of this word by using these examples and your dictionary.

204. TO OBSTRUCT

Here are two examples of potential use;
1. A large tree **obstructed** the road
2. She was charged with **obstructing** police.

Try to find the meaning of this word and more uses in the dictionary.

REVIEW: 28

This is the answer to the exercise.

Choose the best word for the following definitions:

1. Possible to be easily broken or damaged.
   a. Fever
   b. To notice
   (c) Fragile

2. To seize temporarily or permanently as way of penalty for use.
   a. Technique
   (b) Confisicate
   c To notice

3. To ignore (something) or treat (something) as unimportant.
   a. Compliment
   (b) Disregard
   c. To recommend

4. A situation in which many people do not have enough food to eat.
   (a) Famine
   b. Stranger
   c. Economy

5. To think about something unceasingly or persistently.
   a. Rich
   b. Recommend
   (c) Obsess

6. A story that is told or written.
   (a) Narrative
   b. To speak up
   c. To notice

205. PROFICIENT

Here are two examples of potential use;
EX 1. He has become very **proficient** at computer programming.
EX 1. She is **proficient** in two foreign languages.

Have a great weekend and happy English learning!

206. OBSTINATE

Here are two examples of potential use:
Ex 1. Terorism is a very **obstinate** problem facing the world.
Ex 2. My parents remain as **obstinate** as ever.

Try to find the meaning of this word by using these examples and your dictionary.

REVIEW: 29

Review your vocabulary with this exercise.

Fill in the gaps with the correct form of the following words;

**REMOTE   INVOLVE   FACILITATE   OBSTRUCT
PROFICIENT OBSTINATE**

1. He told us a story _____ life on a farm.
2. A piece of food _____ his airway and caused him to stop breathing.
3. She became very _____ in her old age.
4. The moderator's role is to _____ the discussion by asking appropriate questions.
5. He is an _____ child with a violent temper.
6. He shows a high level of _____ in Spanish.

207. OBSTACLE

Here are two examples of potential use;
1. He overcame the **obstacles** of poverty and neglect.
2. They must overcome a number of **obstacles** before the restaurant can be opened.

Try to find the meaning of this word and more uses in the dictionary.

208. IMPRESS

Here are three examples of potential use;
1. I am **impressed** that you can play the violin so well.
2. The speaker tried to *impress* the dangers of drugs *on* the children.
3. A design was *impressed* on the book's cover.

Try to find the meaning of this word and more uses in the dictionary.

209. OUTBREAK

Here are three examples of potential use;
1. There was an **outbreak** of violence and war in the northern part of Africa.
2. They are preparing for an **outbreak** of the virus.

Try to find the meaning and more uses in the dictionary.

Treasure box: Think in English.
This takes some getting used to, but soon you will find it becoming a second nature; the right words or phrases will come faster and easier then.

210. TO BOOST

Here are three examples of potential use;
1. The company needs to find ways to **boost** [=*improve*] morale.
2. She **boosted** the boy onto his father's shoulders.

Try to find the meaning and more uses in the dictionary.

REVIEW: 29

Fill in the gaps with the correct form of the following words;

**REMOTE   INVOLVE   FACILITATE   OBSTRUCT
PROFICIENT OBSTINATE**

1. He told us a story ＿＿ **involving** ＿＿ life on a farm.
2. A piece of food ＿＿ **obstructed** ＿＿ his airway and caused him to stop breathing.
3. She became very ＿＿ **remote** ＿＿ in her old age.
4. The moderator's role is to ＿＿ **facilitate** ＿＿ the discussion by asking appropriate questions.
5. He is an ＿＿ **obstinate** ＿＿ child with a violent temper.
6. He shows a high level of ＿＿ **proficient** ＿＿ in Spanish.

211. ABSTRACT

Here are two examples of potential use;
1. Data for the study was **abstracted from** hospital records.
2. Personal problems **abstracted** him so persistently.

Look it up in the dictionary and see other ways of using it.

212. ELIGIBLE

Here are three examples of potential use;
1. I'd like to vote but I'm not *eligible* yet.
2. He won't be *eligible to retire* until next year.

Try to find the meaning and more uses in your dictionary.

REVIEW: 30

Check your vocabulary with this exercise.

Fill in the space with the appropriate form of the following words.

OBSTACLE, IMPRESS, OUTBREAK, BOOST, ABSTRACT, ELIGIBLE

1. There was an immediate _____ of paper shuffling and a pretense of work when the supervisor passed through the room.
2. Honesty, truth and justice are _____ words.
3. The are working hard to _____ the value of money on their children.
4. It has been more than six years since the fall of the Taliban, fewer than 30% girls are _____ to enroll in schools.
5. Lack of experience is a major _____ for her opponent.
6. The article discusses a number of ways people can _____ their immune systems.

213 REPLY

Here are three examples of potential use;
1. I called out to them, but no one **replied.**
2. He **replied** politely that he felt a little better.

Try to find the meaning and more uses in the dictionary.

214. "LEARN THE ROPES"

Meaning: If you learn the ropes, you learn how to do a job properly, or how to get things done.

For example:
1. Karen will teach you what to do, and it shouldn't take you too long to **learn the ropes.**
2. It can take quite a while for a new lawyer to **learn the ropes** in a big legal firm.

215. TO EXCLAIM

Here are two examples of potential use:

Ex 1. She **exclaimed** in delight over the Christmas tree.

Ex 2. The children **exclaimed** with wonder when they saw the elephant.

Try to find the meaning of this word by using these examples and your dictionary.

216. FOUND

Here are two examples of potential use:

Ex 1. The well diggers **found** a number of Native American artifacts.

EX 2. After an hour of searching, I finally **found** my glasses

Try to find the meaning of this word by using these examples and your dictionary.

REVIEW: 30

Check your vocabulary with this exercise.

Fill in the space with the appropriate form of the following words.

OBSTACLE, IMPRESS, OUTBREAK, BOOST, ABSTRACT, ELIGIBLE

1. There was an immediate _____ **outbreak** _____ of paper shuffling and a pretense of work when the supervisor passed through the room.
2. Honesty, truth and justice are _____ **abstract** _____ words.
3. They are working hard to _____ **impress** _____ the value of money on their children.
4. It has been more than six years since the fall of the Taliban, fewer than 30% girls are _____ **eligible** _____ to enroll in schools.
5. Lack of experience is a major _____ **obstacle** _____ for her opponent.
6. The article discusses a number of ways people can _____ **boost** _____ their immune systems.

How many did you get right? Don't worry if you missed some, try next time.

217. BEGGAR

Here are two examples of potential use:
EX 1. He's a lazy **beggar**.
EX 2. Pitiful **beggars** are such a common sight in underdeveloped countries.

Look it up in your dictionary and try to understand by using these examples.

218. REPLACE

Here are two examples of potential use:
Ex 1. Will computers ever completely **replace** books?
EX 2. She was hired to **replace** the previous manager.

Try to find the meaning of this word by using these examples and your dictionary.

REVIEW: 31

Check your understanding of the words we have learned with this exercise.

The doorbell rang, and the housewife answered it. She found two beggars outside. "So, you're begging in twos now?!" she exclaimed.

"No, only for today," one of them replied. "I'm showing my replacement the ropes before going on holiday."

Make the best choice.

1. A 'beggar' is a person who _____
   a. Sells food and clothes
   b. has no money
   c. asks for money
   d. does the housework

2. To 'exclaim' means to _____
   a. say something kindly
   b. say suddenly and loudly
   c. walk quickly
   d. look angrily

3. A _____ is a person that you put in place of yourself or another.
   a. beggar
   b. rope
   c. housewife
   d. replacement

4. 'Ropes' here means _____
   a. the rules and customs in a place or activity
   b. pieces of strong thick cord
   c. people you probably meet in a special place
   d. houses which are expensive

5. 'Reply' means _____
   a. to take someone for a ride
   b. to ignore someone
   c. to respond in words or writing
   d. to make a loud noise

6. 'found' here means
   a. to invent something
   b. to gain or regain the use or power of something
   c. to be determined
   d. to come upon or see often accidentally

219. DIMENSION

Here are two examples of potential use:
Ex 1. She carefully measured each *dimension* of the room.
EX 2. Please, do not underestimated the *dimensions* of this problem.

Try to find the meaning of this word by using these examples and your dictionary.

220. CONTRAST

Here are two examples of potential use:
Ex 1. Her black dress *contrasts* sharply *with* the white background.

EX 2. We compared and **contrasted** the two characters of the story.

Try to find the meaning of this word by using these examples and your dictionary.

221. TO INFECT

Here are two examples of potential use:
Ex 1. If you're sick you should stay home to avoid *infecting* other people in the office.
EX 2. Her enthusiasm has *infected* everyone.

Try to find the meaning of this word by using these examples and your dictionary.

222. LEGIBLE

Here are two examples of potential use:
Ex 1. She has a **legible** handwriting.
EX 2. The document is not **legible**.

Try to find the meaning of this word by using these examples and your dictionary.

Here is the answer to **Review: 31**

Beggar Replacement

The doorbell rang, and the housewife answered it. She found two beggars outside. "So, you're begging in twos now?!" she exclaimed.

"No, only for today," one of them replied. "I'm showing my replacement the ropes before going on holiday."

Make the best choice.

1. A 'beggar' is a person who _____
    a. sells food and clothes
    b. has no money
    c. asks for money
    d. does the housework

2. To 'exclaim' means to _____
    a. say something kindly
    b. say suddenly and loudly
    c. walk quickly
    d. look angrily

3. A _____ is a person that you put in place of yourself or another.
    a. beggar
    b. rope
    c. housewife
    d. replacement

4. 'Ropes' here means _____
    a. the rules and customs in a place or activity
    b. pieces of strong thick cord
    c. people you probably meet in a special place
    d. houses which are expensive

5. 'Reply' means _____
    a. to take someone for a ride
    b. to ignore someone
    c. to respond in words or writing
    d. to make a loud noise

6. 'found' here means
    a. to invent something
    b. to gain or regain the use or power of something
    c. to be determined
    d. to come upon or see often accidentally

How many did you get right?

223. SUSPECT

Here are two potential use;
EX 1. He's **suspected** of involving in four burglaries.
EX 2. Call the doctor immediately if you **suspect** you've been infected.

224. TRAUMA

Here are two examples of potential use:
Ex 1. She never fully recovered from the *trauma* of her experiences.
EX 2. The accident victim sustained multiple *traumas.*

Try to find the meaning of this word by using these examples and your dictionary.

REVIEW: 32

Use the correct form of these words to fill in the gaps;

DIMENSION, CONTRAST, INFECT, LEGIBLE, SUSPECT, TRAUMA

1. The _____ vehicle was reported to the police.
2. They were unable to prevent bacteria from _____ the wound.
3. His essay _____ his life in America with/to life in India.
4. She never fully recovered from the _____ she suffered during her childhood.
5. He doesn't write _____ at all and it is very difficult to read his writings.
6. The social/political/religious _____ of the problem must also be taken into account.

225. KNOB

Here are two examples of potential use'
EX 1. The left **knob** [=dial] controls the volume.
EX 2. The **knob** [=doorknob] is stuck and I can't open the door!

Try to understand the meaning through these examples and look it up in your dictionary.

Treasure box: Observe the mouth movements of those who speak English well and try to imitate them. When you are watching television, observe the mouth movements of the speakers.

Repeat what they are saying, while imitating the intonation and rhythm of their speech.

226. AWARE

Here are two examples of potential use;
1. I was not fully **aware** of the danger.
2. Students today are very **aware** about the environment.

Try to find the meaning of this word and more uses in the dictionary.

227. SEMICIRCLE

Here are two examples of potential use;
1. The children sat in a **semicircle**.
2. The houses are built in a **semicircle**.

Try to find the meaning of this word and more uses in your dictionary.

228. LOUNGE

Here are two examples of potential use'
EX 1. There were not enough seats in the **lounge** for all the guests.
EX 2. The hotel has a television **lounge**.

Try to understand the meaning through these examples and look it up in your dictionary.

REVIEW: 32

Here is the answer to the exercise to review our vocabularies.

Use the correct form of these words to fill in the gaps;

DIMENSION CONTRAST INFECT LEGIBLE SUSPECT TRAUMA

1. The _____ **suspect** _____ vehicle was reported to the police.
2. They were unable to prevent bacteria from _____ **infecting** _____ the wound.
3. His essay _____ **contrasts** _____ his life in America with/to life in India.
4. She never fully recovered from the _____ **trauma** _____ she suffered during her childhood.
5. He doesn't write _____ **legibly** _____ at all and it is very difficult to read his writings.
6. The social/political/religious _____ **dimensions** _____ of the problem must also be taken into account.

How did you do?

229. FUMBLE

Here are two examples of potential use,
EX 1. He **fumbled** (around) for the light switch when she woke up in the middle of the night.
EX 2. She **fumbled** with her keys as she tried to unlock the door.

Try to understand the meaning through these examples and look it up in your dictionary.

230. RESIDENT

Here are two examples of potential use,
EX 1. Several tribes are **resident** in this part of the country.
EX 2. She is a **resident** of New York. [=she lives in New York].

Try to understand the meaning through these examples and look it up in your dictionary.

Treasure box: Listen to the 'music' of English.
Do not use the 'music' of your native language when you speak English. Each language has its own way of 'singing'.

REVIEW: 33

The Story

Staying at a hotel in Kawaguchi, I couldn't sleep because the television in the residents' lounge was so loud. As I could see from the top of the stairs, the lounge was in total darkness, so I crept downstairs in my pajamas. I went to the TV and after some fumbling with the knobs I managed to switch it off.

As I turned to leave, I suddenly became aware of a semi-circle of people sitting in the dark who, up until that moment, had been enjoying a television program.

Mark the best choice.

1. 'Lounge' is _____
   a. kind of taxi in the airport etc.
   b. small room for workers
   c. public sitting room in a hotel
   d. special case for television

2. To 'creep' means to _____
   a. run quickly
   b. jump off
   c. shout out
   d. move quietly

3. To '_____' means to move the hands awkwardly to do something or to find something.
   a. fumble
   b. manage
   c. switch
   d. reside

4. A 'knob' is a _____
   a. hotel room
   b. small TV
   c. round handle
   d. special table

5. Aware here means _____
   a. to manage
   b. having knowledge or conscious
   c. to switch
   d. to jump into something

6. Resident means _____
   a. One who resides in a particular place permanently or for an extended period.
   b. a public living room
   c. anyone who uses management skills or holds the organizational title
   d. continuing or enduring without fundamental or marked change

7. Semi circle means _____
   a. a prolonged exposure to the sun
   b. record of some proceedings
   c. a half of a circle
   d. The way houses are built.

231. ENSURE

Here are two examples of potential use;
EX. 1 They took steps to *ensure* the safety of the passengers.
EX. 2 We want to *ensure* [=make certain/sure] that it doesn't happen again.

Try to look it up in your dictionary for more understanding of the meaning.

232. PREVENT

Here are two examples of potential use;
EX. 1   Seatbelts in cars often *prevent* serious injuries.
EX. 2   He grabbed my arm to *prevent* me *from* falling.

Try to look it up in your dictionary for more understanding of the meaning.

233. TO BAN

Here are two examples of potential use;
EX. 1   The city has *banned* smoking in all public buildings.
EX. 2   He was *banned from* entering the building.

Try to look it up in your dictionary for more understanding of the meaning.

234. GUILTY

Here are two examples of potential use;
EX. 1 Do you think he's innocent or *guilty?*
EX. 2 The children exchanged *guilty* looks.

Try to look it up in your dictionary for more understanding of the meaning.

235. INSTANT

Here are two examples of potential use;
EX. 1 He became an *instant* celebrity with the publication of his first novel.

EX. 2 The Internet provides *instant* access to an enormous amount of information.

Try to look it up in your dictionary for more understanding of the meaning.

REVIEW: 33

Here is the answer to the exercise for this.

The Story

Staying at a hotel in Kawaguchi, I couldn't sleep because the television in the residents' lounge was so loud. As I could see from the top of the stairs, the lounge was in total darkness, so I crept downstairs in my pajamas. I went to the TV and after some fumbling with the knobs I managed to switch it off.

As I turned to leave, I suddenly became aware of a semi-circle of people sitting in the dark who, up until that moment, had been enjoying a television program.

Mark the best choice.

1. 'Lounge' is _____
   (C) Public sitting room in a hotel.

2. To 'creep' means to _____
   a. run quickly
   b. jump off
   c. shout out
   (d). move quietly

3. To '_____' means to move the hands awkwardly to do something or to find something.
   (a). fumble
   b. manage
   c. switch
   d. reside

4. A 'knob' is a _____
   a. hotel room
   b. small TV
   (c). round handle *
   d. special table

5. Aware here means _____
   a. to manage
   (b). having knowledge or conscious*
   c. to switch
   d. to jump into something

6. Resident means _____
   (a). One who resides in a particular place permanently or for an extended period.
   b. a public living room
   c. anyone who uses management skills or holds the organizational title
   d. continuing or enduring without fundamental or marked change

7. Semi circle means _____.
   a. a prolonged exposure to the sun
   b. record of some proceedings
   (c). a half of a circle*
   d. The way houses are built

236. AGONY

Here are two examples as usual of potential use;
EX 1. She was in terrible **agony** after breaking her leg.
EX 2. The medicine relieves the **agony** of muscle cramps very quickly.

Look it up in the dictionary for the meaning and more use.

REVIEW: 34

Match the following words with the correct definitions.

ENSURE, PREVENT, GUILTY, AGONY, INSTANT, BAN

1. A very short period of time.

2. To forbid (someone) from doing or being part of something.

3. Extreme mental or physical pain.

4. Responsible for committing a crime or doing something bad or wrong.

5. To stop someone or something from doing something.

6. To make (something) sure, certain, or safe.

237. TO OBJECT

Here are two examples of potential use;
EX. 1 No one *objected* when the paintings were removed.
EX. 2 He *objected* that the chair was too big to fit in the car.

Try to look it up in your dictionary for more understanding of the meaning.

238. WEIRD

Here are two examples of potential use;
EX. 1 She listens to some really *weird* music.
EX. 2 My little brother acts *weird* sometimes.

Try to look it up in your dictionary for more understanding of the meaning.

239. TO ADAPT

Here are two examples of potential use;
EX. 1 When children go to a different school, it usually takes them a while to *adapt*.
EX. 2 The camera has been *adapted* for underwater use.

Try to look it up in your dictionary for more understanding of the meaning.

Answer toReview: 34

Match the following words with the correct definitions.

ENSURE, PREVENT, GUILTY, AGONY, INSTANT, BAN

1. A very short period of time . . . . **Instant.**
2. To forbid (someone) from doing or being part of something . . . **Ban.**
3. Extreme mental or physical pain . . . . **Agony.**
4. Responsible for committing a crime or doing something bad or wrong . . . **Guilty.**
5. To stop someone or something from doing something . . . **Prevent.**
6. To make (something) sure, certain, or safe . . . **Ensure.**

240. MASSIVE

Here are two examples of potential use;
EX. 1 A *massive* effort will be required to clean up the debris.
EX. 2 He suffered a *massive* heart attack .

Check it out in your dictionary for more understanding of the meaning.

241. ENFORCE

Here are two examples of potential use;
EX.1. Police will be enforcing the parking ban.
EX.2. This is not an enforceable contract.

Check the meaning up in the dictionary for more understanding of how to use.

242. SIGNIFICANT

Here are two examples of potential use;
EX. 1 A *significant* number of customers complained about the service.
EX. 2 He won a *significant* amount of money. .

Check it out in your dictionary for more understanding of the meaning.

REVIEW: 35

Match the following words with the appropriate definition.

ADAPT, MASSIVE, ENFORCE, SIGNIFICANT, WEIRD, OBJECT

1. To impose (a course of action) upon a person or a group of people is _____
2. To make suitable to requirements or conditions; adjust or modify fittingly is _____
3. To express or feel disapproval, dislike, or distaste is _____

4. Large in scale, amount, or degree is _____
5. Important or having or likely to have influence or effect is _____

6. of strange, odd or extraordinary character is _____

243. RESEARCH

Here are two examples of potential use;
EX. 1 Recent *research* shows that the disease is caused in part by bad nutrition.
EX. 2 He did a lot of *research* before buying his car.

Check it out in your dictionary for more understanding of the meaning.

244. TOPIC

Here are two examples of potential use;
EX. 1 He is comfortable discussing a wide range of *topics*.
EX. 2 The new boss has been the main *topic of* conversation.

Check it out in your dictionary for more understanding and uses.

245. TO AID

Here are two examples of potential use;
EX. 1 He jumped into the water to *aid* the drowning child.
EX. 2 His research *aided in* the discovery of a new treatment for cancer.

Check it out in your dictionary for more understanding and uses.

Treasure box: Don't give up!
Some students say" I've been studying for 3, 4,5 years, but still I can't speak well".My advice is, to continue learning and you may try various ways of doing it to avoid boredom. You can always start all over again and again, even going back to the basic

246. TO DELEGATE

Here are two examples of potential use;
EX. 1 A manager should *delegate* authority to the best employees.
EX. 2 He *was delegated* by the town to take care of the monument.

Check it out in your dictionary for more understanding and uses.

REVIEW: 35

Here is the answer to the exercise to review your vocabulary.

Match the following words with the appropriate definition.

ADAPT, MASSIVE, ENFORCE, SIGNIFICANT, WEIRD, OBJECT

1. To impose (a course of action) upon a person or a group of people is _____ **to enforce** _____
2. To make suitable to requirements or conditions; adjust or modify fittingly is _____ **to adapt** _____
3. To express or feel disapproval, dislike, or distaste is _____ **to object** _____
4. Large in scale, amount, or degree is _____. **to be massive** _____
5. Important or having or likely to have influence or effect is _____ **to be significant** _____
6. of strange, odd or extraordinary character is _____ **to be weird** _____

247. MANDATORY

Here are two examples of potential use;
EX. 1 This meeting is **mandatory** for all employees. [=all employees must go to this meeting].
EX. 2 The **mandatory** fine for littering is $200. [=everyone caught littering must pay $200].

Check it out in your dictionary for more understanding and uses.

248. ADDICTION

Here are two examples of potential use;
EX.1   He has an *addiction to* playing the lottery.
EX. 2 He devotes his summers to his surfing *addiction*.

Check it out in your dictionary for more understanding and uses.

REVIEW: 36

Here is another exercise to review your vocabulary.

Match the following words with the appropriate definition.

RESEARCH, TOPIC, AID, MANDATORY, ADDICTION, DELEGATE

1. Required or commanded by authority; obligatory _____
2. To assign or entrust responsibility or authority to another _____
3. The collecting of information about a particular subject _____
4. Someone or something that people talk or write about _____
5. To provide what is useful or necessary_____
6. A strong and harmful need to regularly have something or do something _____

249. TREATMENT

Here are three examples of potential use;

EX.1 We want to ensure equal *treatment* for everyone.

EX. 2 Previous *treatments* of this topic have ignored some key issues.

EX. 3 The patient required immediate medical *treatment*.

Check it out in your dictionary for more examples and understanding.

250. UNDERGROUND

Here are three examples of potential use;
EX.1 I've ridden on the New York subway, the Paris Metro, and the London **Underground.**
EX. 2 The drugs are supplied through an ***underground*** network.
EX. 3 They had been living **underground** as fugitives.

Check it out in your dictionary for more examples and understanding.

251. TO VANISH

Here are three examples of potential use;
EX.1 The missing girl ***vanished*** without a trace a year ago.
EX.2 The custom has all ***vanished.*** [=the practice is very rare now].

Check it out in your dictionary for more examples and understanding.

252. NOMINEE

Here are two examples of potential use;
EX.1 She is one of the ***nominees for*** Best Actress.
EX.2 He is the President's ***nominee for*** Attorney General.

Check it out in your dictionary for more examples and understanding.

REVIEW: 36

Here is the answer to the exercise to review your vocabulary.

Match the following words with the appropriate definition.

RESEARCH TOPIC AID MANDATORY ADDICTION DELEGATE

1. Required or commanded by authority; obligatory _____ **mandatory** _____
2. To assign or entrust responsibility or authority to another _____ **to delegate** _____
3. The collecting of information about a particular subject _____ **to research** _____
4. Someone or something that people talk or write about _____ **a topic** _____
5. To provide what is useful or necessary _____ **to aid** _____
6. A strong and harmful need to regularly have something or do something _____ **addiction** _____

253. TO REVIVE

Here are two examples of potential use;
EX. 1 The doctors were trying to *revive* the patient.
EX. 2 The family is trying to *revive* an old custom.

Try to look up the meaning in your dictionary for more understanding.

254. PROPOSAL

Here are two examples of potential use;

EX.1 The committee is reviewing the *proposal* for the new restaurant.

EX.2 They rejected/accepted/considered/approved my business *proposal*.

Check it out in your dictionary for more examples and understanding.

REVIEW: 37

Here is a new exercise to review your vocabularies.

Match the following words with the appropriate definitions.

TREATMENT, UNDERGROUND, VANISH, NOMINEE, REVIVE, PROPOSAL

1. To disappear, especially suddenly or mysteriously.
2. To bring back or to return to life or consciousness.
3. The act, manner, or method of handling or dealing with someone or something.
4. A person or organization named to act on behalf of someone else.
5. Something offered as new offerings for investors included several index funds.
6. Hidden or concealed or relating to an organization involved in secret or illegal activity.

255. FLEXIBLE

Here are two examples of potential use;
EX.1 She's been doing exercises to become stronger and more *flexible*.
EX.2 Whatever you want to do is fine with me, I'm *flexible*.

Check it out in your dictionary for more examples and understanding.

256. IMPAIR

Here are two examples of potential use;
EX.1 Smoking can *impair* your health.
EX.2 The disease causes *impaired* vision/hearing in elderly people.

Check it out in your dictionary for more examples and understanding.

257. CHAOS

Here are two examples of potential use;
EX.1 The loss of electricity caused *chaos* throughout the city.
EX. 2 When the police arrived, the street was in total/complete/absolute *chaos*.

Check it out in your dictionary for more examples and understanding.

258. FUNCTION

Here are two examples of potential use;
EX.1 He believes that the true *function* of art is to tell the truth.
EX. 2 His job combines the *functions* of a manager and a worker.

Check it out in your dictionary for more examples and understanding.

REVIEW: 37

Here is the answer to the exercise.

Match the following words with the appropriate definitions.

TREATMENT, UNDERGROUND, VANISH, NOMINEE, REVIVE, PROPOSAL

1. To disappear, esp suddenly or mysteriously. **VANISH**
2. To bring back or to return to life or consciousness. **REVIVE**
3. The act, manner, or method of handling or dealing with someone or something. **TREATMENT**
4. A person or organization named to act on behalf of someone else. **NOMINEE**
5. something offered as new offerings for investors included several index funds. **PROPOSAL**
6. Hidden or concealed or relating to an organization involved in secret or illegal activity. **UNDERGROUND**

How did you do?

259. RENOWN

Here are two example of potentil use;
EX. 1 That Italian restaurant is **renowned** for its wine list.
EX. 2 He is a **renowned** scientist.

260. SUBSEQUENT

Here are two examples of potential use;
EX.1 Her work had a great influence on ***subsequent*** generations.
EX. 2 She graduated from college and ***subsequently*** moved to New York.

Check it out in your dictionary for more examples and understanding.

Treasure box: Set goals, something that you are trying to do or achieve with English. This will surely motivate you.

REVIEW: 38

Here is a review of the words we learned.

The words in **bold** are in the wrong places, put them in the appropriate places.

1. The action for which a person or thing is particularly fitted or employed. **CHAOS**
2. Following in time or order; succeeding. **IMPAIR**
3. Capable of being bent repeatedly without injury or damage. **FUNCTION**
4. To cause to diminish, as in strength, value, or quality. **SUBSEQUENT**
5. The quality of being widely honored and acclaimed; fame. **FLEXIBLE**
6. A condition or place of great disorder or confusion. **RENOWN**

261. TO OBTAIN

Here are two examples of potential use;
EX.1 The information may be difficult to *obtain*.
EX. 2 They've *obtained* the necessary permission to enter into the house.

Check it out in your dictionary for more examples and understanding.

262. ABSTAIN

Here are two examples of potential use;
EX.1 I need to **abstain** from eating for at least 12 hours before my blood test.
EX. 2 People are **abstain** from (drinking) alcohol when they drive.

Check it out in your dictionary for more examples and understanding.

263. GENERATE

Here are two examples of potential use;
EX.1 This business should **generate** a lot of revenue.
EX.2 They have been unable to **generate** much support for their proposals.

Check it out in your dictionary for more examples and understanding.

264. PROFESSIONAL

Here are two examples of potential use;
EX.1 Do you have any *professional* experience?
EX.2 Her presentation was very *professional*.

Check it out in your dictionary for more examples and understanding.

Review: 38
Here is the answer to the review of the words.

The words in **bold** are in the wrong place, put them in the aproprite place.

1. The action for which a person or thing is particularly fitted or employed. **FUNCTION**

2. Following in time or order; succeeding. **SUBSEQUENT**
3. Capable of being bent repeatedly without injury or damage. **FLEXIBLE**
4. To cause to diminish, as in strength, value, or quality. **IMPAIR**
5. The quality of being widely honored and acclaimed; fame. **RENOWN**
6. A condition or place of great disorder or confusion. **CHAOS**

265. STUMBLE

Here are two examples of potential use of stumle;
EX. 1 She usually **stumbles** out of bed [=gets out of bed] around 7:00 am.
Ex. 2 The economy has *stumbled* in recent months.

Find the meaning in the dictionary and more examples.

266. NEGLIGENCE

Here are two examples of potential use;
EX.1 The company was charged with **negligence** in the manufacturing of the defective tires.
EX.2 Medical *negligence* may be the cause of Michael Jackson's death.

Check it out in your dictionary for more examples and understanding.

REVIEW: 39

Let's review our vocabularies with this exercise.

Fill in the gaps with the appropriate form of the following words.

OBTAIN ABSTAIN GENERATE PROFESSION STUMBLE NEGLIGENCE

1. Higher education always seems to _____ controversy.
2. The horse _____ and almost fell.
3. These ideas no longer _____ for our generation.
4. The downfall of the company was brought about by many _____ of the staff.
5. He desided to _____ from taking part in the discussion.
6. I was impressed by the calm and _____ way she handled the crisis.

Here are the answers to the review questions

Fill in the gaps with the **appropriate form** of the the following words.

OBTAIN ABSTAIN GENERATE PROFESSION STUMBLE NEGLIGENCE

1. Higher education always seems to _____ **generate**_____ controversy.
2. The horse _____ **stumbled** _____ and almost fell.
3. These ideas are no longer _____ **obtainable** _____ for our generation.

4. The downfall of the company was brought about by many _____ **negligence** _____ of the staff.

5. He desided to _____ **abstain** _____ from taking part in the discussion.

6. I was impressed by the calm and _____ **professional** _____ way she handled the crisis.

267. UNLIKELY

Here are two examples of potential use;

EX.1 It is *unlikely* that the company will survive more than another year.

EX.2 A big city is an unlikely place to find wildlife.

Check it out in your dictionary for more examples and understanding.

268. DILUTE

Here are two examples of potential use;

EX.1 You can dilute the medicine with water.

EX.2 The hiring of the new CEO diluted the power of the company's president.

Check it out in your dictionary for more examples and understanding.

269. TO BOND

Here are two examples of potential use;

EX.1 We were strangers at first, but we bonded (*with* each other) quickly.

EX.2 The pieces of wood bonded (to each other) well.

Check it out in your dictionary for more examples and understanding.

270. TO GAMBLE

Here are two examples of potential use;

EX.1. She thought starting her own business was a gamble so she gave up the idea.

EX.2. Many people are willing to *take a* gamble on the new medical treatment. [=to try the new treatment.

Check it out in your dictionary for more examples and understanding.

271. TO NEGOTIATE

Here are two examples of potential use;

EX.1. Teachers are negotiating for higher salaries.

EX.2. The driver carefully negotiated the winding road.

Check it out in your dictionary for more examples and understanding.

REVIEW: 40

Let's see how much we've learned.

Write one word with the same meaning to each of the following words.

1. UNLIKELY _____
2. TO DILUTE _____
3. TO BOND _____
4. TO GAMBLE _____
5. ASSET _____
6. TO NEGOTIATE _____

272. TO MANIPULATE

Here are two examples of potential use;

EX.1. The program was designed to organize and *manipulate* large amounts of data.

EX.2. She knows how to manipulate her parents to get what she wants.

Check it out in your dictionary for more examples and understanding.

273. TO INTIMIDATE

Here are two examples of potential use;

EX.1. He is one of the most intimidating men I have ever met.

EX.2. I feel less intimidated now than I did when I started the job.

Check it out in your dictionary for more examples and understanding.

274. SYNONYM

Here are three examples of potential use;
EX.1 "Small" is a synonym of "little".
EX.2 Can you think of a synonym for "original".
EX. 3 He is a tyrant whose name has become a synonym for oppression.

Check it out in your dictionary for more examples and understanding.

275. ANTONYM

Here are two examples of potential use;
EX.1 "Hot" and "cold" are antonyms.
EX.2 Fast is an antonym of slow.

Check it out in your dictionary and compare with synonym.

Treasure box: Treat yourself for a job well done after you studied well and continue to do it. This will also motivate you.

Answer to Review: 40.

Here are the posible answers to the review.

Write one word with the same meaning to each of the following words.

1. UNLIKELY _____ Not likely; improbable. Not promising; likely to fail.
2. TO DILUTE _____ weaken, adulterate, decrease, lessen
3. TO BOND _____ fix, hold, bind, connect, glue, stick, paste, fasten

4. TO GAMBLE _____ take a chance, back, speculate, bet.

5. ASSET _____ benefit, help, service, aid, advantage, strength

6. TO NEGOTIATE _____ bargain, manage, debate, discuss.

276. TO COMPENSATE

Here are two potential uses
EX. 1 She was compensated for the loss of her arm in the accident.
EX. 2 Management compensated us for the extra time we worked.

Try and check your dictionary for more understanding.

277. SPECIFIC

Here are two examples of potential use;
EX.1 Is there anything specific you want for dinner?
EX.2 We were each given a specific topic to talk about.

Check it out in your dictionary for the meaning and more examples.

REVIEW: 41

Let's review the words the we learned.

Give the synonyms and antonyms of the following words

	WORDS	SYNONYMS	ANTONYMS
1.	MANIPULATE	....	....
2.	INTIMIDATE	....	....
3.	SYNONYM	....	....
4.	ANTONYM	....	....
5.	COMPENSATE	....	....
6.	SPECIFIC	....	....

278. TO DISCOVER

Here are two examples of potential use;
EX.1 It took her several weeks to discover the solution.
EX.2 During her career she was responsible for *discovering* many famous musicians.

Check it out in your dictionary for the meaning and more examples.

279. TO PERCEIVE

Here are two examples of potential use;
EX.1 The detective perceived [=saw] a change in the suspect's attitude.
EX.2 He is perceived as one of the best players in baseball.

Check it out in your dictionary for the meaning and more examples.

280. TO MANIFEST

Here are two examples of potential use;
EX.1 Both sides have manifested a stubborn unwillingness to compromise.
EX.2 Love manifests [=reveals] itself in many different ways.

Check it out in your dictionary for the meaning and more examples.

281. TO EXIST

Here are two examples of potential use;
EX.1 She believes that ghosts really do exist.
EX.2 Does life exist on Mars?

Check it out in your dictionary for the meaning and more examples.

Answer to Review: 41

WORDS	SYNONYMS	ANTONYMS
1. MANIPULATE	use	Leave alone
2. INTIMIDATE	buly	encourage
3. SYNONYM	equivalent	antonym
4. ANTONYM	opposite	synonym
5. COMPENSATE	refund	deprive
6. SPECIFIC	definite	uncertain

282. EFFECTIVE

Here are two examples of potential use;
EX.1 It's a simple but effective technique.

EX. 2 He gave an effective speech.

Look it up in the dictionary for the meaning and more examples.

283. CIRCUMSTANCE

Here are two examples of potential use;
EX.1 The circumstances of his death are suspicious.
EX.2 Due to circumstances beyond our control, the flight is canceled.

Check it out in your dictionary for the meaning and more examples.

REVIEW: 42

Here is a new exercise to review our vocabularies.

Match the words with the appropriate definitions

DISCOVER PERCEIVE MANIFEST EXIST EFFECTIVE CIRCUMSTANCE

1. To notice, think or become aware of something or someone is

   _____

2. The way something happens : the specific details of an event is

   _____

3. To see, find, or become aware of something for the first time is

   _____

4. To continue to be or to live or to be real _____
5. Easy to understand or recognize or visible _____
6. Producing a result that is wanted or having an intended effect

   _____

284. TRADITIONAL

Here are two examples of potential use;
EX.1 It is traditional to eat turkey and cranberry sauce on Thanksgiving.
EX.2 She loves wearing traditional Japanese kimono for special occasion.

Check it out in your dictionary for the meaning and more examples.

Answer to Review: 42.

DISCOVER PERCEIVE MANIFEST EXIST EFFECTIVE CIRCUMSTANCE

1. To notice, think or become aware of something or someone is **to perceive**
2. The way something happens : the specific details of an event is **to be circumstance**
3. To see, find, or become aware of something for the first time is **to discover**
4. To continue to be or to live or to be real **to exist**
5. Easy to understand or recognize or visible **manifest**
6. Producing a result that is wanted or having an intended effect **effective**

285. PARTICIPATE

Here are two examples of potential use;

EX.1 Most people joined the game, but a few chose not to participate.

EX.2 He is known for his active participation in community affairs.

Check it out in your dictionary for the meaning and more examples.

286. HENCEFORTH

Here are two examples of potential use;

EX.1 Henceforth, supervisors will report directly to the manager.

EX.2 She announced that henceforth she would be running the company.

Check it out in your dictionary for the meaning and more examples.

287. ENCOUNTER

Here are two examples of potential use;
EX.1   We encountered problems early in the project.
EX.2   The pilot told us that we might encounter turbulence during the flight.

Check it out in your dictionary for the meaning and more examples.

288. IGNITE

Here are two examples of potential use;
EX. 1   The fire was ignited by sparks.
EX. 2   Three wins in a row ignited the team.

Try to check the meaning up in your dictionary for more examples and understanding.

289. TIMID

Here are two examples of potential use;
EX.1   she's very timid and shy when meeting strangers.
EX.2   He gave her a timid smile.

Check it out in your dictionary for the meaning and more examples.

290. MOMENTUM

1.   The strength or force that something has when it is moving.
2.   The strength or force that allows something to continue or to grow stronger or faster as time passes.

Examples;

*The truck gained momentum [=it moved faster] as it rolled down the hill.
* The truck lost momentum [=it slowed down] as it rolled up the hill.
*The company has had a successful year and hopes to maintain its momentum by introducing new products.

Look it up in a dictionary for more meaning and more examples

Treasure box: Read aloud in English for 15-20minutes every day. Research has show it takes about three months of daily practice to develop strong mouth muscles for speaking a new language. Start with very simple books, even children books will help you.

291. HAMMAR

Meanings;
1. As a noun it means a tool that has a heavy metal head attached to a handle and that is used for hitting nails or breaking things apart.
2. As a verb it means (a.) to strike blows especially repeatedly with. (b) to make repeated efforts especially to reiterate an opinion or attitude.

Examples;
*John, please get me my new hammer to nail these pieces of wood together."
*The sound of the rain hammering the metal roof of our camper made sleeping nearly impossible.

Look it up in the dictionary for more understanding and more examples.

292. BEGINNING

1. Meanings as a noun with potential examples
   a. The point or time at which something begins or a starting point.
   EX. He has been working there since the beginning of the year.

   b. The first part of something.
   Ex. Go back to the beginning of the song.

2. Meaning as an adjective with potential examples.
   To start learning the simple or basic parts of a subject.
   Ex. The school has courses for beginning [=elementary], intermediate, and advanced students.

293. RESOLUTION

Meanings and Examples;
1: The ability of a device to show an image clearly and with a lot of detail
   A high-resolution copier/monitor/camera/computer.

2: A promise to yourself that you will make a serious effort to do something that you should do.
   a. He made a resolution to lose weight.
   b. Her New Year's resolution is to exercise regularly.

Please look it up in your dictionary for more meanings and examples of how to use this it

294. HIT

MEANINGS;
a. When used as a verb, this word means to strike.

b. When it's used as a noun, however, it means a big success.

EXAMPLES
a. When children are young, they have to be taught not to **hit** other children.
b. The new book about William and Catherine's wedding is sure to be a big hit

Try to look it up in your dictionary for more examples.

295. SAFETY

- As noun it means free from danger or risk of injury.
- It can also be used as an adjective when describing a characteristic of something which provides safety.

Examples;
a. It's very important to learn about safety before handling and using power tools.
b. He always wears safety glasses when working with chemicals.

Look it up in your dictionary for more understanding and more examples.

REVIEW: 43

Let's review this week's vocabularies with this exercise.

Give the Synonyms and antonyms of these words.

		SYNONYM	ANTONYM
1.	RESOLUTION	....	....
2.	BEGINNING	....	....
3.	HIT	....	....
4.	HAMMER	....	....
5.	SAFETY	....	....
6.	MOMENTUM	....	....
7.	TMID	....	....
8.	IGNITE	....	....
9.	ENCOUNTER	....	....
10.	HENCEFORTH	....	....
11.	PARTICIPATE	....	....
12.	TRADITIONAL	....	....

296. PRESUMPTUOUS.

MEANING: Excessively bold or overconfident.

Examples;

a. They couldn't believe how **presumptuous** their neighbor was in assuming that she was invited to their party.

b. Ever since he was a little child, he had been known to be **presumptuous**, forcing his way into any situation which caught his eye.

c. The **presumptuous** doctor didn't even bother to explain to me the treatment that I would be receiving.

297. OCCUPY.

MEANING;

To fill or be in a place or space or to fill or use an amount of time.

EXAMPLES
1. They have occupied the apartment for three years.
2. That family trip occupies [=*has*] a special place in my memory.
3. Studying occupies nearly all of my time on the weekends.

Look it up in a dictionary for more understanding and more examples.

298. SOLITARY

MEANING,
1. It means, living, or going alone or without companions.
2. One who lives or seeks to live a lonely life.

EXAMPLES
a. He took a solitary walk on the beach.
b. He's a very solitary man.
c. The prisoner was kept in solitary.

299. EMPHASIZE

MEANING

To give special attention to something.

EXAMPLES
a. Their father always emphasized the importance of discipline.
b. He tried to emphasize that he hadn't meant to offend anyone.

Look it up in your dictionary for more understanding and more examples.

300. IMMEDIATE

MEANING
1. Happening or done without delay.
2. Having no other person or thing in between.

EXAMPLES
1. The new restaurant was an immediate success.
2. They have evacuated everyone in the immediate area of the wildfire.
3. Hospital visits are limited to immediate family.

Look it up in your dictionary for more understanding and more examples.

Here is the answer to the review 43.

		SYNONYM	ANTONYM
1.	RESOLUTION	. . . STRONG DECISION	. . . FRUSTRATION . . .
2.	BEGINNING	. . . . COMMENCEMENT	. . . TERMINAL . . . .
3.	HIT	. . . . AFFECT, SUCCEED	. . . MISS . . .

4.	HAMMER	. . . . REPEAT	. . . . WITHDRAW
5.	SAFETY	. . . . SECURITY	. . . . INECURITY . . .
6.	MOMENTUM	. . . . IMPULSE	. . . SLOW . . . .
7.	TMID	. . . FEARFUL	. . . . BRAVE . . .
8.	IGNITE	. . . START UP	. . . . QUENCH . . .
9.	ENCOUNTER	. . . . CONFRONTAION	. . . RETREAT . . .
10.	HENCEFORTH	. . . FROM NOW	. . . PRECEDE . . .
11.	PARTICIPATE	. . . . JOIN IN	. . . OBSERVE . . . .
12.	TRADITIONAL	. . . . COMMON	. . . . . NEW . . . .

301. OFFER.

MEANING.
1. To give someone the opportunity to accept or take something or to say that you are willing to do something.
2. To say or express (something) as an idea to be thought about or considered.

EXAMPLES
a. I'd like to offer a couple of comments on the points you've raised.
b. The victims were offered money as compensation for their injuries.

302. EXTEND

MEANING
1. To become longer or to be able to become longer or to make (something) longer or greater.
2. To offer (feeling, such as an apology) to someone.

EXAMPLES
a. The table measures eight meter long when it is fully extended.

b. She extended her visit by a couple of weeks.
c. They extended a warm welcome to us.

Look it up in your dictionary for more understanding and more examples.

303. REGULATE

MEANING
1. To set or adjust or control the amount, degree, or rate of something.
2. To bring something under the control of authority or government.

EXAMPLES
a. The thermostat regulates the room's temperature.
b. We need better laws to regulate the content of the Internet.
c. The government regulates foreign trade.

Look it up in a dictionary for more understanding and more examples.

304. SHATTER

MEANING;

To break or be broken into many small pieces.

EXAMPLES;
1. The windshield shattered when the bullet went through the glass.
2. Reading about all the necessary paperwork and licenses needed before opening a business, shattered his entrepreneurial dreams.

Look it up in a dictionary for more meanings and examples.

305. LAMENT

MEANING

To express grief or deep regret about something or action.

EXAMPLES;
a. They lamented the fact that they didn't study harder in school.
b. She may unfortunately have to lament her carelessness for a long time.

Look it up in a dictionary and make your own sentences for more understanding.

Treasure box: Be curious, have interest and desire to learn more. Use every opportunity to learn, such as on the train, in the restaurant, change the signs from your language to English.

306. FLAMBOYANT

MEANING.

Having a very noticeable quality that attracts a lot of attention.

EXAMPLES
a. A flamboyant performer was at the station.
b. The flamboyant gestures of the conductor attracts people's attention.
c. A lot of models wearing flamboyant clothes were at the show.

Look it up in a dictionary for more examples.

307. COMMUNITY.

MEANINGS

1. A group of people who live in the same area such as a city, town, or neighborhood.
2. A group of people who have the same interests, religion, race, etc.
3. A group of nations—usually singular.

EXAMPLES

a. The festival was a great way for the local community to get together.
b. An artistic/business/medical community.
c. The international community .

Look it up in a dictionary for more examples.

REVIEW: 44

Let's review our vocabularies.

Fill the following gaps with the appropriate form of the following words.

PRESUMPTUOUS SOLITARY OCCUPY, EMPHASIZE, IMMEDIATE, OFFER, EXTEND, REGULATE, SHATTER, LAMENT, COMMUNITY, FLAMBOYANT

1. She _____ herself with her butterfly collection.
2. Dr. Jones _____ exercise in addition to a change in diet.
3. Paul was a shy, pleasant _____ man, his evenings were spent in _____ drinking.
4. Relief agencies say the _____ problem is not a lack of food, but transportation.
5. The situation _____ us opportunities to learn.
6. The governor found it _____ that the mayor called him by his first name.
7. Live animal research is more tightly _____ in Britain than anywhere else in the world.
8. Fodak recruits, trains and support _____ based volunteers to work in the _____ with disadvantaged groups and individuals.
9. Payne took very full advantage of the invitation _____ by his cousin, who wanted somebody to cheer him up.
10. On really bad days Mae would come home absolutely _____
11. They were all very _____ women, very well dressed with lots of jewelry.
12. You always hear aspiring authors _____ about finding the time to write.

308. REMAIN

MEANINGS

It means to stay in the same place or with the same person or group or to stay behind or unchanged.

Examples;
a) Only a little remained after the fire.
b) I remained behind after the class had ended.
c) Organic remains are good source of energy.

Look it up in a dictionary for more possible use and meanings.

309. TOGETHER

Here are possible meanings and uses.

1. To be with each other.
   The old friends were together again after many long years apart.
2. In or into one group, mixture, piece, etc.
   They gathered together to celebrate.
3. When people are in a close relationship.
   They've been together for almost five years.
4. When two or more people or things touch.
   The doors banged together.
5. When things happen at the same time.
   They all cheered together.

Look it up in a dictionary for more understanding.

310. BEAUTY

MEANINGS and potential uses.

1. The quality of being physically attractive.
   * Her beauty is beyond compare.

2. A good or appealing part of something.
   *The beauty of the game is that everyone can play.

311. SPECIFIC

Here are the meanings and potential use.

1. Special or particular
   * Is there anything specific you want for dinner?
2. Clearly and exactly presented or stated.
   *The doctor gave the patient specific instructions on how to take the medication.

Look it up in a dictionary for more understanding.

312 ATTRACTIVE

Here is the possible meaning and some potential use.

A very pleasing appearance or quality that people like.

a. An attractive woman greeted us at the door.
b. The camera has many attractive features at a very attractive price.

Look it up in your dictionary for more meanings and examples.

Answer to Review 44

Fill the following gaps with the appropriate form of the words.

PRESUMPTUOUS, SOLITARY, OCCUPY, EMPHASIZE, IMMEDIATE, OFFER, EXTEND, REGULATE, SHATTER, LAMENT, COMMUNITY, FLAMBOYANT

1. She _____ occupies _____ herself with her butterfly collection.
2. Dr. Jones _____ emphasizes _____ exercise in addition to a change in diet.
3. Paul was a shy, pleasant _____ solitary _____ man, his evenings were spent in _____ solitary _____ drinking.
4. **Relief agencies say the _____ immediate _____ problem is not a lack of food, but transportation.**
5. The situation _____ offers _____ us opportunities to learn.
6. The governor found it _____ presumptuous _____ that the mayor called him by his first name.
7. Live animal research is more tightly _____ regulated _____ in britain than anywhere else in the world.
8. Fodak recruits, trains and support _____ community _____ based volunteers to work in the _____ community _____ with disadvantaged groups and individuals.
9. Payne took very full advantage of the invitation _____ extended _____ by his cousin, who wanted somebody to cheer him up.
10. On really bad days Mae would come home absolutely _____ shattered _____
11. They were all very _____ flamboyant _____ women, very well dressed with lots of jewelry.
12. You always hear aspiring authors _____ lament _____ about finding the time to write.

313. BROAD.

Here are the meanings and some examples;
1. Large or wide from one side to the other.

He has broad shoulders.

2. Including or involving many things or people.
   The store has a broad selection of coats

3. Concerning the main parts of something.
   The broad outlines of a problem.

Look it up in your dictionary to help you understand more

314. PURCHASE

Here is the meaning and some potential use;

it means to get obtain (something) by paying money for it.

It is a formal word for the word "**buy**".

a. He purchased a new suit for one hundred dollars.
b. Souvenirs can be purchased at the gift shop.

Look it up in the dictionary for more meanings and understanding.

315. PRIVILEDGE.

Here are the meanings and possible uses;
1. A right or benefit that is given to some people and not to others.
   *Good health care should be a right and not a privilege.
2. A special opportunity to do something that makes one proud.
   * Meeting the President was a privilege.

Look it up in a dictionary for more understanding.

316. REQUIREMENT.

Here is the meaning and possible use;
Requirement is something that is needed or that must be done.
He has met the basic or minimum requirements for graduation.
Look it up in a dictionary for more meanings and understanding.

317. SADDLE

Here are the meanings and possible use.
As a noun, it means a leather-covered seat that is put on the back of
a horse or a seat on a bicycle or motorcycle.
As a verb, it means to put a saddle on a horse.

a. He saddled his horse and mounted it.
b. He saddled up his horse.

318. AGILE.

Here are the meanings and possible examples;

Agile means to be able to move quickly and easily, quick, smart,
and clever.

a. She is the most *agile* athlete on the team.
b. Leopards are very fast and agile.

Look it up in a dictionary for more understanding.

319. AFFIRM.

Here are the meanings and some potential use;

1. To affirm means, to say that something is true in a confident way

   We cannot *affirm* that this painting is genuine.

2. It can also mean to decide that the judgment of another court is correct.

   The decision was affirmed by a higher court.

Please look it up in the dictionary for more understanding.

REVIEW: 45

Let's review our vocabularies with this exercise.

SECTION A.

Find the synonyms and antonyms of these words

WORDS	SYNONYMS	ANTONYMS
1. REMAIN	....	....
2. TOGETHER	....	....
3. BEAUTY	....	....
4. SPECIFIC	....	....
5. ATTRACTIVE	....	....
6. BROAD	....	....

SECTION B

These vocabularies in bold are wrongly used, correct them.

1. He's **agile** to serve in Margaret Thatcher's cabinet.
2. I need to **privilege** a new heavy coat.
3. Although he was very big he was incredibly **purchase** and elegant.
4. What are the basic entry **affirm** for the course?
5. We cannot **saddle** that this paint is genuine.
6. The company is **requirement** with an enormous amount of debt.

320. COMPATIBLE

Here are the meanings and possible use.

It is the ability to exist together without trouble or conflict or going together well.

a.   My roommate and I are very compatible.
b.   This printer is compatible with most PCs.

Look it up in the dictionary for more understanding.

Treasure box: Pronounce the ending of each word. Pay special attention to 'S' and 'ED' endings. This will help you strengthen the mouth muscles that you use when you speak English.

321. RECEPTIVE.

Here is the meaning and some potential use.

Receptive means to be willing to listen to or accept ideas, suggestions, etc.

a.   I was happy to be speaking before such a *receptive* audience.
b.   He was receptive *to* the idea of going back to school.

Look it up in the dictionary for more understanding.

322. BREAKTHROUGH.

Here the meaning and potential use.

Breakthrough means a person's first important success after trying for a long period of time.

a. Researchers say they have achieved a major breakthrough in cancer treatment.

b. This job could be the breakthrough she's been waiting for.

Look it up in a dictionary for more understanding.

323. ADORE.
Here are the meanings and potential use;
1. To adore means to love or admire someone very much.
   * She adores her son.
   *He's a good doctor. All his patients adore him.

2. It also means to like or desire something very much or to take great pleasure in something.
   He adores [=*loves*] chocolate.

Look it up in the dictionary for more understanding.

324. PASSIONATE.

Here is the meaning and potential use;

To be passionate is, having, showing, or expressing strong emotions or beliefs for or toward something or someone.

*She has a *passionate* interest in animal rights.
*She is *passionate* about art/music/sports/healthy living.

Look it up for more understanding in a dictionary.

325. NOSTALGIA

Meaning;

Nostalgia is the pleasure and sadness that is caused by remembering something from the past and wishing that you could experience it again.

Example;

A wave of nostalgia swept over me when I saw my childhood home.

Look it up in a dictionary for more understanding.

REVIEW: 45

Here is the answer to the exercise.

SECTION A

Find the synonyms and antonyms of these words

WORDS	SYNONYMS	ANTONYMS
1. REMAIN	Stay, Rest, continue	Leave, Depart
2. TOGETHER	With, Join	Solely, Independent
3. BEAUTY	Loveliness, Merit	Merit, Ugliness
4. SPECIFIC	Particular, Precise	General, Overall
5. ATTRACTIVE	Appealing	Unattractive
6. BROAD	Expansive, Wide	Narrow

SECTION B:

1. He's **privilege** to serve in Ronald Regan's cabinet.
2. I need to **purchase** a new heavy coat.
3. Although he was very big he was incredibly **agile** and elegant.
4. What are the basic entry **requirements** for the course?
5. We cannot **affirm** that this paint is genuine.
6. The company is **saddled** with an enormous amount of debt.

326. QUITE

Meaning;

Quite means to a very noticeable extent or completely, entirely or exactly.

It is used to express agreement.

It is also used to make a statement stronger.

It is used more often in British English than in the U.S. English, but it is not unusual.

Examples; We go out to dinner quite frequently.

* I haven't seen her for quite some time.
* I am quite capable of doing it myself, thank you.
* No one realized quite what was happening.
* "We need to let children be children." "Quite."

Look it up in a dictionary for more understanding.

327. PRETTY

Meaning;

Pretty means to some degree or extent but not very or extremely.

* The house was pretty big.
* The movie was pretty good but not great.
* She was driving pretty fast.

Quite and pretty are very similar in meaning:

* Amanda lives quite near me, so we see each other pretty often.

You can use quite but not pretty in some cases like:

* There were quite a lot of people at the meeting.
Quite goes before a/an
We live in quite an old house.

Compare; *sally has quite a good job.
* Sally has a pretty good job.

Pretty is an informal word and used in spoken English.

Please look it up in a dictionary for more understanding.

328. RATHER.

Rather is similar to quite and pretty. It is often used for negative ideas.

*The weather isn't so good. It's rather cloudy.
*Paul is rather shy, he doesn't talk very much.
* He has been spending rather a lot of money lately.
Quite and pretty are also possible in these examples.
When rather is used for positive ideas, it means "unusually" or "surprisingly".
* These oranges are rather good. Where did you get them?

329. FAIRLY.

Fairly means to a reasonable or moderate extent.
Fairly is weaker than quite/rather/pretty.
If something is fairly good, it is not very good and it could be better.
*My room is fairly big, but I'd prefer a bigger one.
*We see each other fairly often, but not as often as we used to.

Look it up in a dictionary for more understanding.

330. HARDLY.

Possible meanings;
1. It is used to say that something was almost not possible or almost did not happen.
2. It is also used to say that something happened for only a short time.

Examples;
* She was hardly able to control her excitement.
* Hardly a day goes by when I don't think about you.
* The news is hardly a surprise.
Compare with "Not quite"
*They haven't quite finished their meal yet.
*I don't quite/hardly understand what you mean.

331. RELATIVELY.

Meaning;
Relatively means when compared to others that are similar.

Example;
*The car's price is relatively high/low.
*There were relatively few people at the meeting last night.
*This is a pretty good college, relatively speaking.
* We've had a relatively cold winter last year.

Look it up in a dictionary for more understanding.

REVIEW: 46

Review your vocabularies with this exercise.

SECTION A

Write the synonyms and antonyms of the following words.

		SYNONYMS	ANTONYMS
1.	COMPATIBLE	....	....
2.	RECEPTIVE	....	....
3.	BREAKTHOUGH	....	....
4.	ADORE	....	....
5.	PASSIONATE	....	....
6.	NOSTALGIA	....	....

SECTION B

Complete the following sentences using

QUITE, PRETTY, RATHER, FAIRLY, RELATIVELY, HARDLY.

Combine with some of these words (famous, good, hungry, late, noisy, often, old. surprise, a nice day, a lot of traffic, true, different, impossible, cloudy, boring) or your own idea.

1. I'm _____ Is there anything to eat?
2. How are the photographs you took _____ better than usual.
3. I'm surprised you haven't heard of her. she's _____ famous.
4. I go to the cinema _____ -may be once in a month.

5. I don't know when these houses were built, but they are
   _____

6. The weather isn't so good. it's _____
7. I didn't believe at first, but what he said was _____
8. I enjoyed the film, but it was _____
9. The journey took longer than I expected. There was
   _____

10. I'm afraid I can't do what you asked. It's _____
11. You can't compare the two things. They're _____
12. The changes in service have _____ been noticed.

332. ABOUT.

One of the most common ways to use this preposition is to mean concerning.

This book is about Japan.
The movie was about a famous hero.

Another common way to use the word *about* is to mean *approximately.*

I am about 2 Kilometers from home.
I ate about 3 cookies.

Also in some common phrases;

How about a walk in the park?
How about going on a diet?

333. ABOVE

Meanings;
1. bove as a preposition means, in or to a higher place than something.

2. lso it means a greater in number, quantity, or size than something or more than something.

3. t ma also means, having more importance or power than someone.

* He raised his arms above his head.
* We rented an apartment above a restaurant.
* Who is above him in that department?

Common phrases:

Above all;

It is used to introduce the most important point.

*Work hard, be honest, but above all enjoy yourself.
Above average;
*Temperatures were above average all week.

Look it up yourself in a dictionary for more understanding.

334. ACROSS

Across, is a preposition.
One of the most common meanings is "on the other side of".
*"My friend's house is *across* the street from mine."
*"She slid her cup of coffee *across* the table."
Another common meaning is from one side to the other.
*"They built a bridge *across* the river."
*"The horses ran *across* the field."

Look it up in a dictionary for more examples and understanding.

335. ABILITY

Ability is a skill or talent or power to do something.
*"His *ability* to dance was incredible."
*"Some animals have the *ability* to run at speed of 96 kilometers per hour."
*Natural **ability** without education is like a tree without fruit.

Look it up in a dictionary for more understanding and more examples.

Treasure box: Try to understand in content of conversation as a whole. Pick up the ones you understand and try to speak while you check your understanding.

336. CAPABLE

It means, able to do something, having the qualities or abilities that are needed to do something.

* Many new cell phones are capable of connecting to the Internet.
* He is not capable of making those medical decisions himself.
* I don't believe that she's capable of murder.
* A storm is capable of causing widespread destruction.

337. BENEFIT

1. Benefit means a good or helpful result or effect of doing something.
   *A benefit of museum membership is that purchases are discounted.

2. It means money that is paid by a company or by a government when someone dies, becomes sick, stops working etc.

*He began collecting his retirement benefits when he was 65.

3. Something extra such as vacation time that is given by an employer to workers in addition to their regular pay.
*The job doesn't pay much, but the benefits are good.

4. A social event to raise money for a person or cause.
* The school is having/holding a benefit to raise money for a new gymnasium.

REVIEW: 46

Here is the answer to the exercise.

SECTION A

Write the synonyms and antonyms of the following words.

		SYNONYMS	ANTONYMS
1.	COMPATIBLE	adaptable/suitabbe	incompatible/antagonistic
2.	RECEPTIVE	accessible/friendly	insensitive/unfriendly
3.	BREAKTHOUGH	discovery/sudden success	setback/set backward
4.	ADORE	worship/cherish	Hate/abhor/condemn
5.	PASSIONATE	desireous/loving	indifferent/impassionate
6.	NOSTALGIA	fond memories/reminiscence	apathetic/regret/anticipation

SECTION B

Complete the sentences using **QUITE, PRETTY, RATHER, FAIRLY, RELATIVELY, HARDLY.**

Combine with some of these words (famous, good, hungry, late, noisy, often, old. surprise, a nice day, a lot of traffic, true, different, impossible, cloudy, boring) or your own idea.

1. I'm _____ quite/_____ pretty hungry _____ Is there anything to eat?
2. How are the photographs you took? _____ Relatively _____ better than usual.
3. I'm surprised you haven't heard of her. she's _____ quite/ pretty _____ famous.
4. I go to the cinema _____ quite often/ a lot _____ -may be once in a month.

218

5. I don't know when these houses were built, but they are_____ relatively/ fairly old _____

6. The weather isn't so good. it's _____ rather cloudy.

7. I didn't believe at first, but what he said was _____ quite true _____

8. I enjoyed the film, but it was _____ quite/ relatively boring _____

9. The journey took longer than I expected. There was _____ quite a lot of traffic _____

10. I'm afraid I can't do what you asked. It's _____ rather impossible _____

11. You can't compare the two things. They're _____ quite different _____

12. The changes in service have _____ hardly _____ been noticed.

Way to go!

338. BENEFICIARY

1. A person, organization, etc., that is helped by something or someone.

2. A person, organization, etc., that receives money or property when someone dies.

   * She has made the school the sole beneficiary of/in her will.
   * "I am the *beneficiary* of your generosity."
   * Her father named her the beneficiary of his life insurance policy.

Look this word up in your dictionary for more examples and try to understand it.

339. OVER.

It can be used in the same way as "**above**".

Over is used where there is movement from one side to the other.

Also, over is used with a specified measurement or amount.

*I looked out of the window as we flew over Tokyo.
* A notice over the door told us to remove our shoes.
* Children over 12 have to pay the full price. at Tokyo Disney Resort
* In the summer the temperature is often over 30 degrees.

Look it up in a dictionary for more understanding and possible use.

340. AFTER.

1. It means later in time.
   *I'll finish my homework after dinner.
   *After putting his book down, he switched off the light.
   *She didn't get home till after midnight.

2. It also means "next to"
   *Y comes after X.
   *Turn right after the cinema.

3. It also means 'as a result of"
   *We won't be using the airline after all the trouble they caused us.

Now, look it up for more possible use and meanings.

341. GLOVE

This refers to something worn on a person's hand. It has a place for each finger. It is worn either for warmth or protection for the skin.

Every Christmas, she bought her mother a new pair of gloves.

It is a good idea to wear rubber gloves when working with harsh cleaning products.

Look up this easy word for more understanding of the words around it.

342. AGAINST

1. It means in opposition to someone.
2. It is also used to indicate the person or thing that is affected or harmed by something.
3. Also may mean," in competition with someone or something".
   *Everyone was against them.
   *She voted against the proposal.
   *His parents were angry when they learned he had borrowed the car against their wishes.
   *He denies the charges that have been made against him.
   *It's the Yankees against [=versus] the Red Sox tonight.

Look it up in a dictionary for more examples.

343. ALONG

1. Along means, moving on something long such as a river or road
2. Or at a point on something.
   *We walked along a narrow path in the forest.
   *I ran my finger along the edge of the knife.

*You'll find beautiful wild flowers growing along the side of the road.
*The pharmacy is halfway on the left side along the street.

Look it up in your dictionary for more examples.

344. AMONG

1. This word may means, in or through a group of people or things.
   *The disease spread quickly among the students forcing the school to close for two weeks.

2. It also means, in the presence of a group of people.
   * She enjoys spending time at home among [with] family and friends.

3. It may be used to say that a person or thing is part of a larger group.
   * He has many good qualities, among them is his honesty.

4. Also in sharing to each of a group of people.
   * The property was divided equally among the four surviving children.

Look it up in a dictionary for more possible use and make your own sentences.

REVIEW: 47

Here is an exercise for general review of your prepositions.

Choose the best preposition from the brackets to fill in the gaps.

SECTION A

1. I enjoyed walking _____ (round, in, over) the exhibition.
2. Look both ways before you walk _____ (over, across, along) the road.
3. We sailed our boat _____ alongside, along, in)the river.
4. I studied the back of the man _____ (behind, ahead of, beside)me in the queue.
5. Can you balance a book _____ (on to, with, on top of) your head?
6. I couldn't find my name _____ (in, on, throughout) the list.
7. Sally fell _____ (off, over, down) the stairs and hurt her legs.
8. Do you prefer to sleep _____ (on top of, on to, on) your back, your front or your side?
9. There was a CD enclosed _____ (into, inside, in)the back cover of the book.
10. Dave climbed up _____ (on to, on, above) the roof and rescued the kitten.

345. BEYOND.

1. Beyond means, on or to the far side of something or at a greater distance than something.
   *The parking area is just beyond those trees.

2. Something that is beyond you is too difficult for you.

*The job is beyond his ability (the job is too difficult for him).

3. It may be used to say that something cannot be changed, understood, etc.
   *The circumstances are beyond our control.
   *The stories she tells are beyond belief.

4. Something that continues after a period of time, a particular date, age, etc.
   *The program is unlikely to continue beyond next year.

5. It may also mean "in addition to".
   *There were no other problems with the house beyond [besides] the broken window.

Look it up in a dictionary for more meanings and possible use.

346. DUE TO.

A situation is due to if it is caused by something.

Due to may be used the same way as because of.

* Her health problem was due to overwork.
* The train's delays are due to an electrical fault on the train line.
* Classes were cancelled yesterday due to heavy snow.

Look it up in a dictionary for other words used in the same way.

347. CARRY.

This means to take from one place to another.

To hold (your body or your head) in a particular way.

*He's over 80 years old and still carries himself erect/upright like a soldier.
*"I will *carry* the groceries into the house for you."
*"Could you please *carry* the baby for a while so I can rest my back?"

Look it up in a dictionary for more possible use.

348. CAUTION.

Caution *means carefulness* or care taken to avoid danger or risk or a careful attitude or way of behaving.
*"She used extreme caution when driving on the highway for the first time."
*"Please use caution when you put the eggs in the fridge."
*"The teacher used caution when she brought up his daughter's recent bad behavior."
*"You should use caution when operating the electric saw."

Look it up in a dictionary for more understanding and possible use.

349. CHARISMA

Charisma is personal characteristics which make a person able to attract, impress and inspire other people.

*"Because of his *charisma,* more than 200 people always showed up to his meetings."

*"Her *charisma* was one of the things which caused them to offer her the position of manager."
*"They entrusted the care of their children to her because of her *charisma*."

Look up this familiar word in a dictionary for more possible and understanding.

350. EXCLUDE

1. To prevent someone from doing something or being a part of a group.
    *You can share files with some people on the network while excluding others.

2. To leave out something or to not include (something)
    *The prices on the menu exclude tax.

Look it up in a dictionary for more meaning and understanding.

Treasure box: Listen a lot. Listen to real English on TV or Radio and get used to native speakers way of speaking and try to imitate them while you **cook** yours.

Here is answer to review exercise 47.

Choose the best preposition from the brackets to fill in the gaps.

1. I enjoyed walking _____ round _____ (round, in, over) the exhibition.
2. Look both ways before you walk _____ across _____ (over, across, along) the road.
3. We sailed our boat _____ along _____ (alongside, along, in) the river.

4. I studied the back of the man _____ ahead of _____ (behind, ahead of, beside) me in the queue.

5. Can you balance a book _____ on top of _____ (on to, with, on top of) your head?

6. I couldn't find my name _____ on _____ (in, on, throughout) the list.

7. Sally fell _____ down _____ (off, over, down) the stairs and hurt her legs.

8. Do you prefer to sleep _____ on _____ (on top of, on to, on) your back, your front or your side?

9. There was a CD enclosed _____ inside _____ (into, inside, in) the back cover of the book.

10. Dave climbed up _____ on to _____ (on to, on, above) the roof and rescued the kitten.

351. UNTIL.

1. It means up to a particular time.
   It is used to indicate the time when a particular situation, activity, or period ends.
   * I stayed until morning.
   * She will be out of the office until next week.
   * The coupon is good until the end of March.

2. It is also used to indicate the time when something will happen, etc.
   * We don't open until ten.
   * The car won't be ready until tomorrow.

Look this useful word up in a dictionary for more potential use.

352. DESSERT

Dessert is something sweet which is served at the end of a meal (Be careful not to confuse this with desert, such as the Sahara Desert.)
*"Fruit is a very healthy *dessert.*"
*"Some of her favorite *desserts* are cake, cookies, ice cream, pie, and pudding."
*"In the fall, some favorite *desserts* are pumpkin pie, apple crisp and caramel sundaes."

353. FUTILE.

This is a negative word. It means useless, having no result or effect.
*"Defying the law of gravity is *futile.*"
* All our efforts to help him proved futile.
*He realized the futility of trying to continue his journey.
* They made a futile [=vain] attempt to control the flooding.

Look it up in a dictionary for more possible usage.

354. APPEAL.

1. It may mean, to be liked by someone **or** to be pleasing or attractive to someone
    *Pop music *appeals* to a wide variety of people.

2. It may also mean, to ask for something (such as help or support) in a serious way.
    * The government *appealed* to the people to stay calm.

3. It may also mean, to make a formal request for a higher court to review and change decision.
    *She lost the case, but she *appealed* the following month.

Look this word up in a dictionary for more possible use and more understanding.

355. PERCEIVE.

1. To notice or become aware of something.
   * I perceived that she had been crying.
   * The detective perceived [=saw] a change in the suspect's attitude.

2. To think of someone or something as being something stated.
   * She perceived herself as an independent woman.
   * He is perceived as one of the best players in baseball.

Look it up in a dictionary for more possible use and understanding.

REVIEW: 48

Fill the gaps with appropriate prepositions.

1. We live in a little town which is not famous _____ anything.
2. Are you always fond _____ American films?
3. He has been scared _____ heights since his accident
4. The streets will be crowded _____ tourists during the festival.
5. We didn't go on holiday. Jane wasn't very keen _____ leaving her house.
6. Give me the name of the students who were responsible _____ all that noise.
7. Why don't you trust me? Why are you suspicious _____ my intentions?
8. Ask my husband. I am not good _____ repairing things.
9. My mother would hate being dependent _____ anybody.
10. Don't worry. We'll look after you. There's nothing to be scared _____.
11. I am sick of George! He is always short _____ money!
12. Look! His handwriting is very similar _____ mine.
13. He is a very honest man. We don't think he is capable _____ a theft.
14. We weren't interested at all _____ what he was telling about his journey.
15. The message he sent to me was full _____ mistakes.

356. OUTRAGE.

Outrage means, extreme anger or a strong feeling of unhappiness because of something bad, hurtful, or morally wrong.

*Many people expressed outrage at the court's decision.
* Public outrage over the scandal was great.
Look it up in a dictionary for more possible use.

357. IMPULSE.

1. To do something on (an) impulse or on a sudden impulse is to do it suddenly and without thinking about it first.
   *He bought a new camera on impulse.
   *She quit her job on a sudden impulse.

2. An impulse buy/purchase is something that is bought on impulse and that usually is not really needed
   *Shopping with a credit card can lead to impulse buying.

Look it up in a dictionary for more understanding and possible use.

358. WITHOUT.

1. Without means, not having or including (something).
   * Do you take your coffee with or without sugar?
   * Don't leave home without your wallet.

2. It may be used to say that someone is not with or is not involved with another person or group.
   * He went to the store without her.

3. Also may mean, not using (something specified).
   * These cookies are made without flour.

4. It may also mean, not doing something specified.
   * They left without (even) saying goodbye.

Look it up in a dictionary for more examples and possible use.

359. TOLERATE.

1. To allow (something that is bad, unpleasant, etc.) to exist, happen, or be done.
   * Our teacher will not tolerate bad grammar.
   * I can't tolerate that noise.
   * The government cannot tolerate lawlessness.

2. To accept the feelings, behavior, or beliefs of (someone).
   * I don't like my boss, but I have to tolerate him.

Look it up in a dictionary for more possible use.

360. ACCURATE.

1. Accurate means free from mistakes or errors.
   * The model is accurate down to the tiniest details.
   * Her novel is historically accurate.

2. It also means able to produce results that are correct: not making mistakes.
   * He is an *accurate* reporter.
   * The machine is an accurate measuring device.

Look it up for more possible use in a dictionary.

361. BENEATH.

1. In or to a lower position than something or someone.
   * The sky is above us and the earth is beneath us.
   * Just beneath the surface of the water.

2. It may also mean not worthy of (someone) or not good enough for (someone)
   * He won't do any work that he considers beneath him.

Look the word up in a dictionary for more possible use and understanding.

Answer to Review: 48

Fill the gaps with appropriate prepositions.

1. We live in a little town which is not famous ____ for ____ anything.
2. Are you always fond ____ of ____ American films?
3. He has been scared ____ of ____ heights since his accident
4. The streets will be crowded ____ with ____ tourists during the festival.
5. We didn't go on holiday. Jane wasn't very keen ____ in/at ____ leaving her house.
6. Give me the name of the students who were responsible ____ for ____ all that noise.
7. Why don't you trust me? Why are you suspicious ____ of ____ my intentions?
8. Ask my husband. I am not ____ good at ____ repairing things.
9. My mother would hate being dependent ____ on ____ anybody.
10. Don't worry. We'll look after you. There's nothing to be scared ____ of ____.
11. I am sick of George! He is always short ____ of ____ money!
12. Look! His handwriting is very similar ____ to ____ mine.

13. He is a very honest man. We don't think he is capable _____ of _____ a theft.
14. We weren't interested at all _____ in _____ what he was telling us about his journey.
15. The message he sent to me was full _____ of _____ mistakes.

362. DIVERSE.

It means, made up of people or things that are different from each other.

* His message appealed to a diverse audience.
* The group of students is very diverse.
* A diverse group of subjects.

Please look it up in a dictionary for more possible use and more understanding.

363. SOURCE.

1. Someone or something that provides what is wanted or needed.
   * The college had its own power *source*.
   * She has been a great *source* of strength to me.
   * His job is the family's main *source* of income.

2. The cause of something such as a problem.
   * The delays are a *source* *of* concern.
   * The team's bad play has been a *source* *of* disappointment.

3. The beginning of a stream or river of water.
   * The *source* of the Nile is very mall.

Look it up in a dictionary for more possible use.

364. FEATURE.

1. It is an interesting or important part, quality, ability, etc. of something or somebody.
   *This year's models include several new safety *features*.
   * This camera has several *features* that make it easy to use.
   * The car has some interesting new design *features*.

2. **Also** a part of the face (such as the eyes, nose, or mouth)
   * Her eyes are her best *feature*.

3. It also means a movie that is made to be shown in a theater for entertainment.
   * Tonight's *feature* is a new romantic comedy.

4. It can also mean a special story or section in a newspaper or magazine.
   * The paper ran a *feature* on/about urban violence.

Look it up in a dictionary for more possible use and understanding.

365. CUSTOM.

1. It means something made to fit the needs or requirements of a particular person.
   * The new kitchen will have **custom** cabinets.

2. A professional doing work that fits the needs or requirements of a particular person
   * a **custom** furniture shop.

Look up this word in a dictionary for more possible use and /or meanings.

366. RADIANT.

1. Radiant means having or showing an attractive quality of happiness, love, health, etc.
   * She always has a *radiant* smile.
   * She looked *radiant* at her wedding.

2. It means bright and shining.
   *I was impressed by the *radiant* sun.
   *They were fascinated by the *radiant* blue skies.

3. *Also means,* sent out from something in rays or waves that you cannot see
   * *Radiant* heat.
   * *Radiant* energy.

Look this word up in a dictionary for more possible use.

REVIEW: 49

Review with this exercise.

Write the synonyms and antonyms of the following words;

		SYNONYM	ANTONYM
1.	RADIANT	....	....
2.	CUSTOM	....	....
3.	FEATURE	....	....
4.	SOURCE	....	....
5.	BENEATH	....	....
6.	DIVERSE	....	....
7.	ACCURATE	....	....
8.	TOLERATE	....	....
9.	WITHOUT	....	....
10.	IMPULSE	....	....
11.	OUTRAGE	....	....
12.	PERCIEVE	....	....
13.	APPEAL	....	....
14.	FUTILE	....	....
15.	DESSERT	....	....
16.	UNTIL	....	....
17.	EXCLUDE	....	....
18.	CHARISMA	....	....
19.	CAUTION	....	....
20.	CARRY	....	....
21.	DUE TO	....	....
22.	AGAINST	....	....

23. AMONG ....

24. ALONG ....

25. GLOVE ....

26. OVER ....

27. BENEFICIARY ....

28. BENEFIT ....

29. BEYOND ....

30. AFTER ....

Congratulations! You have made it this far, you deserve a big treat!

Remember all the tips in the treasure boxes and this final one on **Speaking**: How do you learn cycling? How do you learn swimming? You learn cycling by cycling and you learn swimming by swimming. **So, Speaking develops by speaking.** You may be making some grammar mistakes in English. You may not be confident. You may feel that your vocabulary is not good enough. But speaking develops your confidence in English. So, I would recommend that you find a native teacher or make friends with native English speakers, speak to as many people as possible in English every day speak or **cook** more and more sentences in English use your dictionary when you are not sure, learn short useful phrases, they will help develop your confidence.

Happy learning!